John Noble

The Queen's Taxes

An Inquiry into the Amount, Incidence and economic Results, of the Taxation of the

United Kingdom

John Noble

The Queen's Taxes
An Inquiry into the Amount, Incidence and economic Results, of the Taxation of the United Kingdom

ISBN/EAN: 9783337168926

Printed in Europe, USA, Canada, Australia, Japan

Cover: Foto ©ninafisch / pixelio.de

More available books at **www.hansebooks.com**

THE QUEEN'S TAXES:

AN INQUIRY INTO THE

AMOUNT, INCIDENCE, & ECONOMIC RESULTS,

OF THE

Taxation of the United Kingdom,

DIRECT AND INDIRECT.

BY JOHN NOBLE.

"The things to be aimed at are wisdom and moderation, not only in granting, but also in the method of raising the necessary supplies; by contriving to do both in such a manner as may be most conducive to the national welfare, and at the same time most consistent with economy and the liberty of the subject."—*Blackstone's Commentaries.*

PREFACE.

THERE are few subjects of greater importance, as affecting the well-being of the community, than Taxation. The financial legislation of the last twenty-seven years has mainly consisted in the removal of injurious taxes. This beneficial process has vastly simplified our Customs Tariff, diminished the interference of the Excise with manufacturing processes, and afforded ample proof of the pernicious effects of fiscal interference with trade.

The probability that the question of Taxation will receive considerable attention, both in and out of Parliament, during the next few years, renders it desirable that the facts of the case should be placed before the public in a compact form. It is the aim of this work to present a complete analysis of the taxes levied for Imperial purposes, compiled from the latest official documents, and dealing separately with each impost in such a manner as to enable the reader to form his own conclusions, as to its merits or demerits, from the most unquestionable evidence.

The four cardinal maxims laid down by Adam Smith, and generally concurred in by subsequent economists, may be thus briefly summed up. 1. Each subject should contribute according to his ability. 2. The time of payment, mode of payment, and amount to be paid, ought to be clearly defined. 3. Every tax ought to be paid at a time convenient to the taxpayer. 4. Every tax ought to be so contrived as to take as little as possible from the pockets of the people beyond the amount it brings into the treasury, and should impose no injurious restrictions upon either trade, industry, or production. An inquiry into any system of taxation necessarily resolves itself into the question as to how far these conditions are complied with. An indispensable preliminary to such inquiry is an accurate knowledge of facts, which it has been the aim of the author of this volume to collect from the various reports and returns throughout which they are scattered,* and to present to his readers in a compact and convenient form.

---

* The first Annual Report of the Commissioners of Inland Revenue being out of print, a new and revised edition, comprising all that is worth preserving of the succeeding annual reports, has been issued. For the references to the First Inland Revenue Report, see the Report for the years 1856 to 1869, issued in 2 vols.

All controversy upon Taxation appears to resolve itself into a consideration of the alleged merits and advantages of Direct and of Indirect Taxation. On the side of the latter there is enlisted the powerful influence of long prescription, supported by a numerous section of economists, who hold, with Mr. McCulloch, that "moderate duties are innocuous if not advantageous." The opponents of Customs and Excise duties, on the contrary, allege that they are uniformly prejudicial in their economic effects, and extravagant in the cost of their collection. In support of this opinion the high authority of the late Richard Cobden may be quoted; who, in 1859, declared that "the man, or the body of men who should be able to abolish Customs and Excise Duties, in this or any other country, would be the greatest possible benefactors of that country." Between these opposing schools, there is a third, which holds that indirect taxation should be removed from all harmless articles of consumption, but retained upon alcohol and tobacco in order to place a check upon their excessive consumption.

It is not the intention of this work to advocate either of these systems of Taxation, but to present a record of facts which will enable its readers to judge for themselves as to the merits of the controversy. No doubt the author's conclusions have been influenced by the opinions he himself entertains. He trusts, however, that his selection and arrangement of facts will be found to have been carefully and impartially conducted, and that the present volume will form a useful manual on the important subject of National Taxation.

CONTENTS.

CHAPTER I.—INTRODUCTION.

Definition of Taxation—Causes of High Taxes—Objects of recent Fiscal Legislation—Importance of Inquiry into Taxation—Intention of the present Work—Principal Sources of Revenue—Analysis of Taxation showing the amount levied by each description of Impost 1

CHAPTER. II—TAXES ON ARTICLES OF CONSUMPTION.

Origin of Customs—Amount collected at different Periods—Origin of Excise—Analysis of Duties of Customs and Excise, and other Taxes on Commodities 6

CHAPTER III.—TOBACCO AND SNUFF.

Rates of Duty—Quantity taxed and Revenue therefrom—Rate of Taxation on Tobacco, and on Cigars—High Duties and Smuggling—Consumption per head at different Periods—Smuggling in 1833—Report of Committee upon Smuggling in 1844—Alleged Decrease of the Practice—Seizures reported—Increase of Smuggling in 1867 and 1868—Result of Enquiries made by the Author at the Principal Seaports—Reasons alleged for the Decrease in Smuggling since 1863—Consumption of Tobacco by the Working Classes—Reports of Commissioners as to Adulteration 9

CHAPTER IV.—SPIRITS AND ARTICLES CONTAINING SPIRIT.

Rates of Duty—Illicit Distillation—Consumption and average Rates of Duty at various Periods—Effect of increasing the Duties—Statistics of Consumption not trustworthy owing to the Practice of Smuggling—Convictions for Illicit Distillation—High Rates of Duty formerly interfered with Manufactures in which Spirits were Employed—Difficulty obviated by the introduction of Methylated Spirit—Consumption and Rates of Duty on Foreign Spirits at various Periods—Increased Consumption of duty-paid Foreign Spirits owing to Equalization of Duty—Decrease in Home Made Spirits—Adulteration fostered by Heavy Duties 18

CHAPTER V.—WINE.

Rates of Duty, Quantity taxed, and Amount produced—Effect of the Methuen Treaty in supplanting French Wines—Rates of Duty at various Periods—Effect of reducing the Duties upon French Wines—Statistics of Consumption of French, Spanish, and Portuguese Wines at different Periods—Proposed Equalization of Duties 31

CHAPTER VI.—Sugar and Articles of which Sugar is an Ingredient.

Sugar largely consumed by the Working Classes—Effect of Protective Duties formerly levied in favour of Colonial Sugars—Rates of Duty, Quantities taxed, and Revenue—Effect of Reduced Duties on Consumption—Controversy between Grocers and Refiners respecting the Duties—Alleged Effect of present Scale in diminishing Production—Importation and Consumption at different Periods—Probable Effect upon Trade of repealing the Duty—A Tax upon Raw Material of certain Manufactures—Grape Sugar—Summary of Arguments against the Sugar Duty 37

CHAPTER VII.—Tea.

Consumption for a long time Stationary—Rates of Duty, 1801 to 1853—The East India Company's Monopoly—Tables of Duty, Importation, and Consumption 1852 to 1868—Tea a necessary to the Poor—Pressure of the Duty on the Lower Class of Teas—Increased Trade with China since the Duty was reduced—Increased Export Trade in Tea—Results that would follow the Repeal of the Duty 50

CHAPTER VIII.—Coffee and Chicory.

Lesson of the Coffee Duty respecting the Effect of Taxation—Duties levied on Coffee, 1801 to the present Time—Import, Consumption, and Export of Foreign and Colonial Coffee, 1841 to 1868—Average Consumption per head during the present Century—History of the Adulteration of Coffee with Chicory—Duties imposed upon Chicory in consequence of the Loss to the Revenue—Effect upon Consumption of Chicory—Sale of Colonial Coffee largely increased since Protective Duties were abolished 55

CHAPTER IX.—Minor Articles.

Cocoa—Consumption—Rates of Duty—Dried Fruit—Rate of Duty, &c.—Patent Medicines—The Government Stamp supposed by Ignorant People to vouch the Merits of these Preparations—Playing Cards—Gold and Silver Plate 64

CHAPTER X.—Malt and its Products, with their Substitutes.

Rates of Duty, 1697 to the Present Time—Effect of Tax upon Consumption—Decrease of Malt in consequence of the rivalry of Tea and Coffee—The Agricultural View of the Malt Tax—Report of the Committee of 1868—Analysis of the Division Lists in the Committee—The Official View of the Malt Tax—Lord John Russell, C. P. Villiers, and Richard Cobden on the Malt Tax—Cost to the Consumer of collecting the Malt Tax—The Moral Argument—Adulteration—Amount of Duty in 1868-9—Foreign Malt—Consumption per Head from 1740—A Substitute for the Malt Tax 68

Contents. xiii

CHAPTER XI.—LICENSES ON TRADES AND PROFESSIONS.

Imposed in some instances for Protection of the Revenue—In others for purposes of Police Regulation—Licenses Levied on Manufacturers—Brewers' Licenses—Proceeds of Hop Duty, 1852-61, and of Brewers' Licenses, 1852 to 1866, showing the Effect of commuting the Hop Duty into a License Tax—Proposal to increase Brewers' License as a Substitute for the Malt Tax—Number of Maltsters and Duty collected—Licenses for Manufacturers of Tobacco, Distillers, Rectifiers, Paper Makers, and Soap Makers—Beer, Spirit, and Wine Dealers' Licenses—Other Licenses 80

CHAPTER XII.—PROBATE, LEGACY, AND SUCCESSION DUTIES.

History of the Probate Duties—Present Scale of Duties—Inequalities of Probate Duties—Levied on Personal Property only—Assessment of Large Estates at Lower Rates than Small ones—Payment of Duty on Full Value, including Debts—Increased cost of Letters of Administration—History of the Legacy Duty—Succession Duty—Rates of Duty—Difference in the Mode of Assessing the Legacy and the Succession Duties—Mr. Bright's Illustration of the Injustice of the Mode in which the Succession Duty is levied—Mr. Gladstone's Defence—Failure of the Succession Duty to realise the Estimated Amount—Opposition of the Landowners to the Succession Duty—An Examination of the Plea for Reduced Assessment on account of the alleged Pressure of Local Rates—Proposed Assessment of Property held by Corporations to an Analogous Tax—Alleged Objection that such Taxes are Paid out of Capital 91

CHAPTER XIII.—MISCELLANEOUS STAMP DUTIES.

Amount Collected under each Head—Changes in the Mode of Collection—Litigation formerly caused by Complexity of the Stamp Duties—Modificationssince 1849—Result of Reducing the Receipt Stamp Duty to a Penny—Objections to the Stamp Duties on Sale and Transfer of Property—Mode in which such Taxes should be assessed—Miscellaneous Stamp Duties—Fees in Courts of Law Collected by Stamps—Objection to Stamp Duty on Marine Insurances—Stamp Duty on Patents for Inventions 111

CHAPTER XIV.—TAXES ON RAILWAYS, SERVANTS, CARRIAGES, HORSES, MULES, DOGS, AND ARMORIAL BEARINGS.

Railway Passenger Duty—Taxes repealed in 1868—Prospect of repeal of the Railway Passenger Tax—Assessed Tax on Dogs, changed to License Duty in 1857—Result of the Change—Present scale of Duties levied upon Servants, Carriages, Horses, and Armorial Bearings—Number of Acts levying Assessed Taxes, wholly or partially repealed in 1868—Exemption of Horses engaged in Agriculture—Objections to these Taxes considered 118

CHAPTER XV.—INHABITED HOUSE DUTY.

History of the House Duty—Exemptions—Opinions of Mr. J. S. Mill and Mr. McCulloch—House Tax partially a tax on Rent of Land—Incidence of the Tax—Objections to the Tax considered 124

CHAPTER XVI.—THE LAND TAX.

Origin of the Land Tax—Abolition of Feudal Tenures and Imposition of Excise Duties in lieu thereof under Charles II—This Transfer accompanied by the introduction of a Standing Army—Conversion of Landholders into Land Owners—Effects of the Change—Taxation in the Reign of Charles II. and James II.—Dissatisfaction with the amount of the burden thrown upon the People—Revision of the Land Tax in the Reign of William and Mary—Assessment of the Tax upon Real and Personal Property—Mode in which Payment of the Tax has been evaded by means of subsequent Legislation—Non-assessment and Relief of Personal Property from the Tax—Plan for redeeming the Land Tax—Probable Result if the Land Tax had been maintained according to the evident intention of the first Act passed in the Reign of William and Mary 135

CHAPTER XVII.—PROPERTY AND INCOME TAX.

History of the Tax from its Introduction in 1798 to the Termination of the French War—Condition of Great Britain and Ireland when it was renewed by Sir Robert Peel—Various Modifications of the Tax since 1842—Amount Collected under each Schedule—Inequality of the Tax as respects Permanent and Precarious Incomes — Exemption of Premiums on Life Policies, &c.—Evidence of Mr. Mill and other Witnesses before Select Committee in 1852 as to Assessment of the Tax 148

CHAPTER XVIII.—INCOME TAX: SCHEDULE A—LANDS, HOUSES, &c.

This Schedule a Tax on Rent—Amount Collected under the following Heads: Lands, Messuages, Manors, Fines—Assessment of Lands in England and Wales at various Periods—Ditto in Scotland—Reasons why the Increase is Larger in Scotland than in England and Wales—Tax on Rent less Prejudicial to Landowners than Customs and Excise—Assessment of Houses at different Periods—Increase in the National Expenditure—The alleged Burdens upon Land—Increased Rental Created by the Common Industry of the Nation a Fair Subject for Special Taxation—Local Burdens upon Land—Special Borrowing Privileges enjoyed by Landowners 158

CHAPTER XIX.—INCOME TAX: SCHEDULE B—OCCUPATION OF LAND.

Assumed Estimate of Farmers' Profits—Special Advantage enjoyed by Farmers over other Traders—Net Rental Assessed at various Periods—Increased Profits of Farmers since 1842 173

Contents.

CHAPTER XX.—INCOME TAX: SCHEDULE C—DIVIDENDS FROM PUBLIC REVENUE.

A Tax on Dividends virtual Repudiation—Justified by Sir Robert Peel because the Fundholder was relieved by means of Income Tax from other Taxes—The Fiscal Policy introduced in 1842 raised the Value of the Funds—Taxation of Foreign Investors—Income Assessed at various Periods—Taxation of Income from Foreign Funds 176

CHAPTER XXI.—INCOME TAX: SCHEDULE D.—PROFITS OF TRADES, PROFESSIONS, AND EMPLOYMENTS.

Increased Assessment in the year 1866 owing to Transfer of Certain Undertakings from Schedule A—Growth of Trading Profits 1814 to 1868—Substitution of the Income Tax for Customs and Excise Duties productive of great Advantage —Opposition to the Tax—Extent to which the Tax is evaded by means of false Returns—Number of Persons assessed at various Amounts—Instances of Evasion, and Mode in which it has been justified by Delinquents—Voluntary Taxation wrong in Principle—Effect of fraudulent returns upon Commercial Morality—Profits of Quarries, Mines, Iron Works, Fisheries, Railways, Gas Works, &c—Assessment under each Head at different Periods .. 179

CHAPTER XXII.—INCOME TAX: SCHEDULE E.—PUBLIC OFFICES AND PENSIONS.

Amount Assessed at different Periods—Certainty of Assessment compared with that of Traders' Profits—Large Increase under this Schedule since 1842-43 196

CHAPTER XXIII.—MODE OF PAYMENT.

" The People must Pay and not Know "—Taxes concealed in Commodities—Dr. Channing on Tariffs—Direct and Indirect Taxes—Convenience as to Mode of Payment may be neutralised by Cost of Collection—Alterations in Payment of Land, House, Income, and Assessed Taxes made in 1869—Taxes repealed in 1869 198

CHAPTER XXIV.—COST OF COLLECTION.

Cost of Collection more Important than Mode of Payment—Direct Taxes involve no Increase beyond the Amount paid to the State—Cost of Collecting Customs—Examination of Statements made by the Comissioners—Cost of Salaries, &c., including Coast Guard—Salaries, &c., Inland Revenue—Increased Cost consequent upon Traders' Profits on Duties advanced—Estimate of Produce Markets Review as to Tea and Sugar—Mr. Fielden, Mr. Cayley, and Sir Fitzroy Kelly as to Malt—Estimate of Mr. Dudley Baxter—Estimate of Mr. G. R. Porter—Sugar—Reasons for believing Increased Cost of Customs and Excise to be at least £10,000,000 205

Contents.

CHAPTER XXV.—CONCLUDING OBSERVATIONS.

Comparative Pressure of Taxation on Real Property, Personal Property, Trade, and Consumption—Difficulty of ascertaining exact Comparative Pressure of Taxes on Consumption—Pressure upon the Working Classes—Opinion of Sir Robert Peel thereon—Effect of Taxes on Commodities upon Trade and Employment—Principles upon which a Revision of Taxation should be Based 219

CHAPTER XXVI.—SUPPLEMENTARY:—THE BUDGET OF 1870.

The Reduction of the Sugar Duties and the Income Tax—Abolition of sundry License Duties—Repeal of Stamp Duty on Hailstorm, Cattle, Boiler, and Plate Glass Insurance—the Gun Tax—Revision of the Stamp Duties—Reduction of Newspaper and Book Postage—Alteration of the Railway Duty—The Brewers' Licences and the Malt Tax—Mr. Lowe on the "Free Breakfast Table" and Direct Taxation. 250

THE QUEEN'S TAXES.

CHAPTER I.

INTRODUCTION.

Taxes are indispensable adjuncts of civilization. They are the premium paid by every citizen to ensure the protection of his person, the security of his property and earnings, and such common advantages as are best attained by the intervention of the Government. In so far as taxes are necessary to secure these ends, they exist on precisely the same footing as rent, premiums of insurance, or any other payment for services rendered. Unfortunately Governments have not been content with the performance of these simple functions, but have involved themselves in needless and extravagant wars, mainly promoted in the interests of ambitious rulers, which have vastly increased the burdens imposed upon their subjects. In consequence of the predominance of this policy during a long period, the taxes now required from the inhabitants of this country are largely in excess of the advantages which the existing government is able to render to its subjects. Hence has arisen that feeling of dissatisfaction with the amount of taxation, which has become an almost recognised privilege of the British subject. If the revenue required to meet our expenditure had been invariably levied on scientific principles, the ill effects of its excessive amount would have been considerably mitigated; this, however, has not been the case; excessive taxation has been levied in the most empirical manner, and the evils of undue expenditure have been thereby aggravated. The financial legislation of the last twenty-seven years has been mainly directed to the removal of these evils, and, as a natural consequence, our fiscal system has, during that period, been completely revised. The present time is, therefore, opportune for a consideration of the existing system of taxation in order that its weight and pressure may be accurately estimated. The levy of taxation is a most important branch of economic science, affecting the well-being of all classes,—consumer, producer, landlord, capitalist, manufacturer, trader, and labourer. Upon the mode in which the public burdens are imposed depends not merely the prosperity, but the very livelihood of large sections of the community. In the following pages it is intended to review, in detail, the fiscal system as it now exists, and to ascertain, as far as possible, in the light of actual facts, the effect of every impost upon the social and economic condition of the people. The fiscal history of the United Kingdom affords abundant material for the task, which it has been the desire of the Author to perform in an impartial spirit, in order that his readers may be able to base their opinions upon facts, and not upon mere theories, however plausible. It will be his aim to throw some light upon the nature, incidence, and effect of the various imposts levied in aid of the Imperial revenue, which, being appropriated for the service of the Crown as the executive power of the commonwealth, are generally known as " the Queen's Taxes."

The following is the gross receipt, and the net produce deducting drawbacks, repayments on over entries, &c., of each of the principal sources of the National Revenue for the year ending March 31st, 1869 :—*

	Gross Receipt.			Net Receipt.†		
	£	s.	d.	£	s.	d.
Customs	22,585,529	0	0	22,422,472	5	11
Excise	21,084,365	8	8¼	20,475,740	7	4¾
Stamps	9,505,238	4	1¼	9,241,450	11	6¼
Taxes	12,242,101	8	9¾	12,110,413	0	2
	£65,417,234	1	7¼	£64,250,076	5	0

Under one or other of the above heads is collected every impost which comes strictly under the definition of a tax levied for the service of the Government. The remaining sources of Income were the revenue from the Post Office, which is a payment for a service

---

* Parliamentary Paper " Taxes and Imposts " Session 1869, No. 427.

† Finance Accounts 1868-9, pp 23-26. The net receipt includes several small charges for special services, fees, fines, &c., not included in the paper from which the gross amount is taken, amounting to £184,729 7s. 8d.

performed by the Government rather than a tax, £1,355,016 13s. 8d.;* the Crown Lands, £446,174;† and miscellaneous receipts from various sources paid into the Exchequer, £3,355,991.‡ The division of the revenue derived from taxation into the four main items of Customs, Excise, Stamps, and Taxes is to a certain extent arbitrary; many imposts are collected by the officers of excise which are not duties levied upon commodities; while under the heads of Stamps and Taxes are included the most varied sources of revenue. It has been necessary, therefore, in order to ascertain the exact proportion raised by each description of tax to re-arrange the details collected under the four main divisions of our Fiscal System. The result is shown in the following table, which presents a summary of the revenue for the year 1868-9, arranged according to the sources from which it was derived :—§

Duties on Articles of General Consumption :—

	£	s.	d.
Customs ‖	22,585,529	0	0
Excise	17,775,695	16	9
Stamps	142,863	3	1¾
Carried Forward	40,504,087	19	10¾

---

* This is net revenue the gross amount was £4,553,580 18s. 2d., the cost of collection, or Post-office Service, being £3,198,564 4s. 6d. Parliamentary Paper, Session 1869, No. 427.

† This is the gross amount received, including £88,206, expenses of management and sundry payments authorized by various Acts of Parliament out of gross revenue before it is paid into the Exchequer. Finance Accounts, 1868-9, p. 15.

‡ Finance Accounts, 1868-9, p. 8.

§ Parliamentary Paper, "Taxes and Imposts," Session 1869, No. 427.

‖ Includes Corn &c., £915,585 repealed in 1869.

The Queen's Taxes.

		£	s.	d.
Brought Forward		40,504,087	19	10¾

Licenses on Trades and Professions :—

	£	s.	d.			
Excise	1,979,729	18	6¼			
Stamps	129,165	0	0			
Taxes	17,746	0	0			
				2,126,641	4	6¼

	£	s.	d.
Probate, Legacy, and Succession duties	4,513,697	14	8½
Stamps on Deeds, Bankers Notes, Bills, Receipts, &c.	3,016,046	5	3¾
Stamps on Law Proceedings	308,192	5	4¼
Marine and Fire Insurances*	1,156,006	14	3

Locomotion :—

	£	s.	d.			
Excise	791,536	16	9¼			
Taxes	844,474	14	1			
				1,636,011	10	10¼

	£	s.	d.
Land Tax	1,131,301	8	2
Tax on Offices and Pensions	19	16	0
Licenses (various) granted for periods less than a year	56,107	13	3¾
Surcharges (various)	40,617	14	4
Licenses to kill Game; Race Horses, and Dogs	510,716	12	0
Marriage Licenses	3,899	0	0
Patents for Inventions	119,380	1	10
Newspaper Stamps	115,987	19	6
Inhabited House Tax	1,131,582	10	0¾
Male Servants	233,654	5	0
Hair Powder and Armorial Bearings	69,820	16	1
Income Tax	8,743,462	10	5
	65,417,234	1	7¼
Post Office	4,553,580	18	2
	£69,970,814	19	9¼

* Fire Insurance £1,070,046 4s. 7d. repealed in 1869.

CHAPTER II.

TAXES ON ARTICLES OF CONSUMPTION.

These imposts which are levied mainly by means of the Customs and Excise form the most important part of the National Revenue. The origin of Customs Duties is somewhat obscure; there appears but little doubt that in one form or another they have existed from a remote period. It is only, however, in modern times that any considerable revenue has been derived from this source. It is probable that originally they were merely small charges upon exports and imports sufficient to defray the cost of maintaining the ports and havens, and to provide for the expense of weighing and measuring goods. The following table shows the proceeds of this branch of the revenue at various periods.*

					£
1596	-	-	-	-	50,000
1613	-	-	-	-	148,075
1660	-	-	-	-	421,582
1689	-	-	-	-	781,987
1712	-	-	-	-	1,315,422
1792	-	-	-	-	4,407,000
1815	-	-	-	-	11,360,000
1843	-	-	-	-	22,647,200
1869	-	-	-	-	22,422,472

* M'Culloch's British Empire, 3rd edition 1847, vol. ii. p 394; First report of Commissioners of Customs 1857, p 106; and Finance Accounts 1868-9, p. 15.

Excise Duties were first levied in the year 1643 by a Parliamentary ordinance, which imposed duties on ale, beer, cider, and perry, and on the makers and vendors thereof. The Royalists soon after followed the example of the Parliament, but the unpopularity of these imposts was so great that both parties pledged themselves to their abolition at the close of the war. In a few years, however, custom had rendered them less intolerable; they were increased, and declared by Parliament, in 1649, to be "the most easy and indifferent levy that could be laid upon the people." From that period they have been continued and have long formed an important branch of the public revenue. The duties imposed upon patent medicines, playing cards, and gold and silver plate, are levied by means of stamps. All these taxes are indirect, being paid in the first instance by the manufacturer or importer, who recovers the amount advanced for duty, with his profit thereon, from the retailer, and ultimately from the customer. The following are the amounts received from these imposts in the year 1868-9, omitting shillings and pence :—*

		£
Tobacco and Snuff :—Customs		6,542,461
Spirits and Articles containing Spirit :—	£	
Customs	4,333,952	
Excise	10,965,195	
		15,299,147
Wine :—Customs		1,523,529
Carried forward		23,365,137

* Parliamentary Paper Taxes and Imposts Session, 1869, No. 127.

Brought forward		23,365,137
Sugar and Articles of which Sugar is an ingredient :—		
Customs	5,743,434	
Excise	71,817	
		5,815,251
Tea :—Customs		2,597,980
Coffee :— do.		357,037
Chicory :—Customs	104,041	
Excise	14,358	
		118,399
Cocoa :—Customs		27,381
Dried Fruit :—Customs		
Currants	268,724	
Figs, Plums, and Prunes	32,994	
Raisins	129,483	
		431,201
Malt and its Products with their Substitutes :—Customs	4,907	
Excise	6,724,323	
		6,729,230
Patent Medicines :—Stamps		66,860
Playing Cards :—		
Customs	338	
Stamps	10,324	
		10,662
Gold and Silver Plate :—		
Customs	3,683	
Stamps	65,678	
		69,361
Corn Meal, &c. :—Customs		915,585
	Total	40,504,084*

* The total, including shillings and pence, is £40,504,087 19s. 10¾d.

CHAPTER III.

TOBACCO AND SNUFF.

This extensively used and much abused article affords an example of a very high rate of taxation, producing a large amount of revenue. The following are the rates of duty, the quantities taxed, and amount of Revenue for the year 1868-69. *

	s.	d.		Quantities Taxed. lbs.	Sum Produced. £
Unmanufactured, containing 10 lbs. or more of moisture in every 100 lbs.	3	$1\frac{3}{10}$ per lb	}	40,197,539	6,327,091
„ containing less than 10 lbs. per 100 lbs.	3	6	„		
Manufactured:—Segars	5	0	„	817,916	204,448
„ Cavendish or Negrohead, of Foreign Manufacture	4	6	„	17,043	3,835
Manufactured in Bond in the United Kingdom	4	0	„	13,752	2,751
Snuff containing more than 13 lbs. of moisture per 100 lbs	3	9	„ }	381	80
" Not containing more than 13 lbs. per 100 lbs.	4	6	„	10,114	Admitted duty free.
Other Manufactured tobacco	4	0	„	21,288	4,259
Total				41,078,033	6,542,464†

* Parliamentary Paper, "Taxes and Imposts," Session 1869, No. 427.

† The total is given in the Parliamentary Paper as £6,542,461; an error of £3 having evidently occurred in the details.

This tax has long been regarded with complacency by Chancellors of the Exchequer, on account of its large yield to the revenue, the ease with which it is collected, and the nature of the article taxed. There are, however, particulars connected with this duty which call for special comment. Foremost is the different rate at which the duty is levied upon the poor man's tobacco and the rich man's cigar. According to the annual statement of trade and navigation for 1868,* the average price in bond in that year was about 7½d.; it appears therefore that the tax upon unmanufactured tobacco is five times the value of the article. If a rich man purchase a pound of cigars worth say 20s., the duty he pays is only 5s., or 25 per cent., while the working man pays 500 per cent. upon his pipe of shag.

In the year ending 31st Dec. 1868, 40,067,329 lbs. of unmanufactured tobacco were entered for home consumption. Of this quantity 27,532,491 was from the United States, and, at the average prices fixed in the annual statement, was worth £856,000, while the duty amounted to £4,333,618, or more than five times the value of the tobacco. In the same year 433,159 lbs. of cigars from Cuba, valued in bond at £259,895, were entered for home consumption, the duty paid on which was £108,288.† If the tax on the cigars from

---

* Annual statement of Trade and Navigation of the United Kingdom with Foreign Countries and British Possessions in the year 1868. Printed by Eyre and Spottiswoode for Her Majesty's Stationery Office, p 20.

† Same, pp 106-7.

Cuba had been assessed at the same rate as that upon the tobacco from the United States, it would have yielded more than £1,300,000 to the revenue.

The high rate of duty levied upon tobacco has frequently been objected to on the ground that it affords encouragement to the practice of smuggling. There can be no doubt that exorbitant duties alone render this practice profitable; one successful venture will reimburse the smuggler for several losses. A return made to the House of Commons for the three years 1843-4-5 showed that 3,011 persons had been convicted during that period. It is, however, impossible to obtain statistics of the number of successful ventures. The Customs Reports of recent years do not disclose any extensive seizures, but they appear to admit the fact that smuggling is a constant practice on board all steamers arriving from foreign countries. The Board of Trade returns show an increased consumption of tobacco, but it is tolerably certain that they do not show the actual quantity consumed at any period. The following table gives the consumption per head of the United Kingdom at several different periods in the present century.*

	oz.		oz.
1801	16·05	1854	16·10
1811	18·44	1861	16·20
1821	11·77	1867	16·35
1831	12·85	1868	16·35
1841	13·36		

---

* Porter's Progress of the Nation, new edition, 1847, p. 575; Statistical Abstract, 1869, pp. 42, 43.

It must not be forgotten that these figures merely include duty-paid tobacco. If the supposition of the Customs authorities, that smuggling has greatly decreased, be correct, the increase in consumption since 1841 is much less than it appears to be from these returns.

The following extract from the *Edinburgh Review* for July 1833, shows the extent to which the practice of smuggling had, at that time, been developed by excessive rates of duty:

"The total quantity of tobacco entered for home consumption in Great Britain and Ireland during the three years ending with 1797, was 53,208,504 lbs.; being at the rate of 17,736,168 lbs. a year. The population of the United Kingdom has more than doubled since 1797, and yet only 20,313,613 lbs. were entered for home consumption in 1832; being 15,000,000 lbs. under what it ought to have been, had the consumption increased proportionally to the increase of population. And that it has done so we have not the slightest doubt; but instead of being wholly supplied, as in 1797, by the free trader, oppressive duties have thrown nearly half the trade of the empire into the hands of the smuggler. The duty in 1797 was 1s. 7d. per lb. in Great Britain, and 8d. in Ireland; and had it been gradually raised in the latter to 1s. 6d. and continued in both countries at that amount, there is every reason to think it would have been more productive than the present duty of 3s. In 1797, no fewer than 8,445,555 lbs. were entered for home consumption in Ireland, whereas, notwithstanding the population has nearly trebled in the interval, only 4,344,764 lbs. were entered in 1832. And yet all those best acquainted with Ireland affirm that the Irish smoke, chew, and snuff, quite as much as ever. The anomaly, however, is apparent only. Their respect for the revenue laws is not such as to make them pay the licensed dealer 3s. 6d. for an article which the smuggler is pressing upon them at 2s. If, as one might be half inclined to suspect, the present exorbitant duty was intended to stimulate the energies and to reward the enterprise of the smuggler, it has had the most perfect success; but, as a fiscal measure, its failure has been signal and complete. 'According,' said Mr. Poulett Thomson in his able speech on the 30th of March, 1830, ' to all accounts laid before the House on this subject, smuggling in this article in England, Ireland, and Scotland, is carried on to the greatest possible extent. I have the fact upon the best authority, that numbers of vessels are constantly leaving the ports of Flushing, Ostend, &c., carrying contraband tobacco to this country; it is a fact, which was established in evidence before a Committee of this House, that *seventy* cargoes of tobacco, containing 3,644,000 lbs., were smuggled in one year on the coast of Ireland, from the port of Waterford to the Giant's Causeway alone. In Scotland smuggling is also carried on to a great extent. The only mode of resisting this system of smuggling consists *in fairly reducing the duty upon the article*. I believe, that were the duty upon it reduced to 1s. or 1s. 6d. per lb. the public would be greatly served, and smuggling put down.'

"The statements of Sir Henry Parnell as to the smuggling of tobacco are exactly similar. It may, therefore, be fairly concluded, that, at the present moment, *half* the tobacco consumed in Ireland, and from a *fourth* to a *third* part of that consumed in Britain, is supplied by the smuggler. And, despite of coast-guards, preventive services, penalties, confiscations, and all the miserable machinery of oppressive taxes, it will continue to be so supplied till 50 per cent. be taken from the duty."

In 1844 a Select Committee of the House of Commons, appointed to consider the state of the tobacco trade, especially in relation to this practice, reported in favour of a " reduction of the high duties as the best means of putting down smuggling." This Committee referred in their report to the opinion of the Commissioners of Excise Inquiry in 1833-4, who recommended as a remedy for the evil, the diminishing the temptation, and added "the nature of this temptation is at once apparent from the fact that £100 expended at

Flushing in buying tobacco may be followed by the receipt of £1,000 if the tobacco can be landed safely in this country." Among the witnesses examined in 1844 was Mr. Ayre, clerk to the magistrates at Hull, who stated his belief, as the result of eight years official experience, that the proportion of detections, compared with successful ventures, was one in fifteen.

It appears from the report of the Commissioners of Customs for the year 1861* to be their opinion that the practice was, at that time, almost annihilated. They say that no organised system then existed for smuggling on a large scale. In subsequent reports they give particulars of numerous seizures, principally, however, of small quantities, concealed in steam boats by the crews. In 1867 † they report an increase of smuggling, mainly in that direction. In the report for 1868 ‡ the Commissioners state that fewer cases appear to have been attempted or discovered in London than in the preceding year, but that there appeared to have been a decided increase at the outports, and that this increase was not in cases which are decided summarily by the magistrates, but in that more important class which are referred to a higher tribunal. The number of cases, including both tobacco and spirits, brought under the notice of the authorities in London in 1868 was about 195 as against 350 in 1867, showing a decrease of 155 cases. In the outports the number of

---

* Sixth Report of the Commissioners of Her Majesty's Customs, 1862, p. 26.

† Twelfth Report of the Commissioners of Customs, 1868, pp. 64-65.

‡ Thirteenth Report of Commissioners of Customs, 1869, pp. 57-59.

seizures, exceeding 10 lbs. in the case of tobacco and 2 gallons in the case of spirits, were 169 in 1868 as against 113 in 1867, an increase of 56. In minor cases there was a decrease of 4, the number being 814 in 1867, and 810 in 1868. Several cases are reported which show the difficulty of preventing smuggling in the case of an article like tobacco, which can be so easily concealed in packages of free goods. In one instance 600 lbs. of tobacco were found concealed in six bales of hops, entered as free goods. In another, 65 lbs. were concealed in a cask of potatoes, whilst 4 lbs. of Cavendish were found ingeniously concealed inside two loaves of baked German bread. It was also made apparent that the sailors in the Royal Navy require watching as well as those in the Merchant Service, 97 lbs. having been seized on board H.M. ship Speedy, 19 lbs. on board H.M. troop ship Crocodile, and 36 bales on board H.M. ship Serapis. The method generally employed in the present day is the concealment of tobacco in packages of duty-paid articles, very ingenious devices being employed for that purpose.*

The result of enquiries made by the author at the principal ports where tobacco is imported fully confirms the statements of the Commissioners. The decrease of the contraband trade is generally attributed to the reduction of duty on manufactured tobacco which took place in 1863, and to the high rate of duty now levied upon Cavendish in the United States, which

---

* Sixth Customs Report, 1862, p. 27 and App., O.

has made that article as dear there as here, and thus stopped much of the smuggling which formerly prevailed. It is still believed that leaf tobacco is smuggled to a considerable extent in Ireland, but that in other respects the practice is pretty well confined to small quantities from the Continent.

Two large seizures were reported to the Commissioners from the north of Ireland in 1868; 13 bales containing 630 lbs. of unmanufactured tobacco at Londonderry, and 948 lbs., with two horses and two carts, at Tralee. In England the principal seizures reported were one of 94 lbs., one of 46 lbs., and one of 136 lbs., in London; 141 lbs. at West Hartlepool; 161 lbs. at Grimsby; and 188 lbs. at Liverpool.

It was stated before a Parliamentary Committee in 1844 that nine-tenths of the tobacco imported into this country was consumed by the working classes. Mr. Dudley Baxter, in his recent work on Taxation, states, as the result of extensive enquiries, that three-fourths of the working men consume tobacco. It must, therefore, be evident that the tax upon that commodity is paid to a large extent by the working men. Opinions vary as to the propriety or necessity of the tax. Some defend it as a restraint upon the consumption of a pernicious indulgence, others as an impost upon a luxury which those who use it can afford to pay. If tobacco be a pernicious indulgence, it is hard to see how the State can with propriety derive any revenue from such a source. If, on the other hand, it is considered a luxury, the question naturally arises as to the policy of placing so heavy a tax upon the luxury of working men, while the many and varied enjoyments of the rich are untaxed. It certainly cannot be said with any show of accuracy that an operative, mechanic, or labourer, who consumes tobacco, is "an untaxed working man."

Another evil which is an invariable attendant of high duties is the encouragement they afford to adulteration. In the last report of the Inland Revenue Commissioners, the Principal of the Laboratory expresses his opinion that this offence has become comparatively rare, but at the same time he states that the practice is kept in check by the frequent inspection of the premises of "those manufacturers who would be disposed to meet fair competition in trade by fraudulent means." It appears, therefore, that tobacco manufacturers carry on their business under strict surveillance.

The number of samples analysed in the year ending 31st March 1867[*] was 206, of which 73 contained illicit ingredients—63 contained liquorice, 11 fermentable sugar, and 4 illicit vegetable matter including rhubarb, cabbage, and exhausted tea leaves. Among other adulterations were caramel, oxide of iron and textile fabric. In the year ending 31st March 1868,[†] 135 samples were analysed, of which 96 were adulterated, the ingredients employed being liquorice, sugar, salt, aniseed, starch, brown paper, and sand.

---

[*] Eleventh Inland Revenue Report App., p xvii.
[†] Twelfth Inland Revenue Report App., p xv.

CHAPTER IV.

SPIRITS AND ARTICLES CONTAINING SPIRIT.

Under this head is collected nearly one-fourth of the entire taxation of the United Kingdom. The following are the present rates of duty, and the quantities taxed and gross produce in 1868-9:—*

Customs:—	Duty. Per Proof Gallon.	Quantities Taxed. Proof Gallons.	Total Gross Produce. £
	s. d.		
Rum and Spirits, of and from British Possessions in America, Mauritius, and the East Indies	10 2	3,817,884	1,940,113
Rum, Foreign, from the country of its production	10 2	54,772	27,843
"not from the country of its production"	10 5	2,390	1,245
Brandy	10 5	3,347,563	1,743,522
Geneva	10 5	134,877	70,253
Other sorts	10 5	1,007,088	524,527
Rum, Shrub, Cordials, &c., from British Possessions in America, Mauritius, and the East Indies	10 2	1,403	713
Other sorts	14 0	36,090	25,300
	per lb.	lbs.	
Chloroform	3 0	921	138
	Per Gallon.	Gallons.	
Collodion	24 0	22	26
Ether	25 0	55	69
Naphtha or Methylic Alcohol (purified)	10 5	—	—
Varnish containing Alcohol	12 0	338	203
Excise:—			
Home Made Spirits	10 0	21,930,393	10,965,195
		Total	£15,299,147

* Parliamentary Paper, Session 1869, No. 427.

The price of Rum in bond, as quoted in the Annual Statement for 1868,* varies from 1s. 9d. to 2s. 8½d. per proof gallon; the average price of French Brandy is 6s. 6d. and of Brandy from Hamburg, Holland, and other parts, 3s. 3d. per gallon. There are no similar returns published as to British spirits; it may, however, be fairly assumed that Gin is about the same value as Rum, and that Whiskey varies considerably according to quality.

There is little doubt that the high rate of duty imposed upon spirits is productive of the usual evils which attend excessive imposts—adulteration, smuggling, and illicit distillation. The problem which successive Chancellors of the Exchequer have endeavoured to solve, in the case of the spirit duties, has been how to raise the largest revenue from the smallest area of consumption without fostering the three evils above-named.

A Table, published by the Inland Revenue Commissioners,† shows that in 1811, with a duty of 2s. 6½d. per gallon, in Ireland 6,378,479 gallons were charged with duty; in 1822, the duty having been raised to 5s. 7¼d., only 2,910,483 were charged. The duty was subsequently reduced to 2s. 4d., and the quantity charged gradually increased till, in 1838, it reached 12,296,342 gallons. It is impossible to arrive at a perfectly accurate estimate of consumption of spirits at different periods, owing to the disturbing

---

* Annual Statement, 1868, pp. 101, 162.
† First Inland Revenue Report, 1857, App., p. 43.

elements of illicit distillation and of smuggling. The following table gives the consumption of duty-paid spirits in the United Kingdom for the years named.*

Year.	Total Consumption. Gallons.	Average Duty.	Consumption per head. Gallons.
1802	15,596,370	6s. 1d.	·98
1821	13,160,288	10s. 4d.	·63
1841	24,106,407	6s. 2d.	·90
1859	28,661,674	8s. 4d.	·80
1868	29,740,314	10s. 1d.	·98

It appears from these figures that the quantity consumed per head is the same now as it was in 1802. We have still, however, to deal with that further unknown quantity, which has paid tribute to neither Customs nor Excise. The Commissioners of Inland Revenue state, in their First Annual Report (1857),† that in the year 1820 illicit distillation had become so prevalent in Scotland and Ireland, that more than half the spirits actually consumed were supplied by the smuggler. An Act was passed in 1823, which reduced the duty from 6s. 2d. in Scotland, and 5s. 7d. in Ireland, to 2s. 4¾d. per imperial gallon for both countries; and new regulations were introduced which combined additional security to the Revenue, with the relief of the distiller from many trammels under which he had previously conducted his operations. In 1825 similar regulations were established in England, and the English duty was reduced from 11s. 8¼d. to 7s. per

---

* Parliamentary Paper, Spirits and Malt, No. 466, Session 1868, Statistical Abstract, 16th No., pp. 41 & 99.

† First Inland Revenue Report, pp. 3-6.

gallon. In consequence of these changes the quantity of duty-paid spirits entered as retained for home consumption was increased from 9,600,000 gallons in 1820, to 18,200,000 gallons in 1826. In the same Report it is said that illicit distillation had always been, more or less, carried on in the large towns of England; and the Commissioners further remark that as illicit spirits can be sold with a fair profit at 5s. or 5s. 6d. per gallon, while the duty on legally made spirits is 8s. (it is now 10s.) per gallon, it cannot be expected that the practice will be easily or entirely suppressed.

In that portion of the First Annual Report, which deals specially with the year 1857, the Commissioners say that in England illicit distillation was then kept within such bounds as not to affect prices in the regular market; that in Scotland it might be said scarcely to exist; but that in Ireland the practice still prevailed to a considerable extent. In the year 1857 the duty was 8s. per gallon in England and Scotland, and 6s. 2d. in Ireland; in 1858 the duty on Irish spirits was advanced to the same rate as on those manufactured in Great Britain, and, in 1860, the duty on all home-made spirits was increased to 10s. per gallon. This measure was followed by a marked diminution in consumption, which the Commissioners of the revenue, however, do not attribute to the increase of illicit distillation. In his budget speech of 1863 Mr. Gladstone expressed his conviction, which he alleged was based on conclusive evidence, that there never had been a period, in recent times, when there had been so little of this practice as during the three previous years. The following table gives the latest returns of the number of convictions.*

Year ending 31st March.	England.	Scotland.	Ireland.
1865	38	9	3,452
1866	41	11	3,557
1867	17	9	2,306
1868	27	11	1,601

Commenting upon the decrease in the number of convictions in Ireland the Commissioners say, "it is probable that the continued high price of barley and oats has had the greatest influence in bringing about this most satisfactory result."

If it be true, as alleged by the Commissioners of Inland Revenue, that illicit distillation, even in Ireland, has been greatly diminished, it is obvious that the returns of consumption previously quoted are not to be relied upon, and that the quantity used has been materially reduced since the commencement of the century. Mr. Dudley Baxter, however, in his recent work on taxation gives expression to his fear that the actual consumption in Ireland is not, as shown by the returns, less than one gallon, but at least a gallon and a half per head. The table on the following page of the quantity of home-made spirits, and the amount of duty, charged in each country shows the result of successive alterations of duty :—†

---

* Tenth Inland Revenue Report, p. 10; Twelfth ditto, p. 7.

† Spirits and Malt Return, Session 1868, No, 466, for the years 1852-56. For the remaining years:—Inland Revenue Reports, 1858, App., p. viii.; 1860, App., p. viii.; 1862, App., p. viii.; 1864, App., p. viii.; 1865, App., p. viii.; 1867, App., p. ix.; 1868, App., p. ix.

	ENGLAND.				SCOTLAND.				IRELAND.		
Years ending	Rate.	Gallons charged.	Amount of Duty.	Rate.	Gallons charged.	Amount of Duty.	Rate.	Gallons charged.	Amount of Duty.		
			£			£			£		
Dec. 31, 1852	7/10	9,820,608	3,816,404	3/8	7,172,015	1,314,869	2/8	8,208,256	1,094,434		
1853	7/10	10,350,307	4,053,970	3/8 4/8	6,534,648	1,433,400	2/8 3/4	8,136,362	1,273,151		
1854	7/10	10,889,611	4,265,097	4/8 5/8 6/	6,553,239	1,806,934	3/4 4/	8,440,734	1,588,745		
1855	7/10 8/	10,384,100	4,090,530	6/ 7/10 8/	5,344,319	1,893,636	4/ 6/ 6/2	6,228,856	1,633,382		
1856	8/	9,343,549	3,737,419	8/	7,715,939	2,870,375	6/2	6,781,068	2,090,829		
Mar. 31, 1857	8/	10,209,731	4,083,892	8/	7,266,867	2,906,746	6/2	6,877,156	2,120,456		
1858	8/	10,995,312	4,398,124	8/	7,024,950	2,809,980	6/2	6,783,871	2,091,693		
1859	8/	10,221,263	4,088,505	8/	6,876,345	2,750,538	6/2 8/	6,101,376	2,338,624		
1860	8/ 10/	10,845,407	4,311,728	8/10	7,429,859	2,973,383	8/ 10/	6,709,926	2,685,643		
1861	10/	9,508,002	4,469,740	..	5,816,835	2,750,781	..	4,822,987	2,269,860		
1862	10/	8,891,625	4,415,817	..	6,124,643	3,062,323	..	4,929,512	2,464,787		
1863	10/	8,876,855	4,438,428	..	6,292,771	3,146,386	..	4,591,256	2,295,628		
1864	10/	8,835,727	4,417,864	..	6,703,256	3,351,628	..	4,692,143	2,346,071		
1865	10/	9,165,781	4,582,891	..	7,131,877	3,565,939	..	4,941,208	2,470,604		
1866	10/	9,214,529	4,607,268	..	7,421,421	3,710,711	..	5,403,266	2,701,634		
1867	10/	9,285,645	4,642,823	..	7,783,915	3,891,972	..	6,057,261	3,028,631		
1868	10/	9,170,562	4,585,283	..	7,144,145	3,572,073	..	6,377,650	3,188,825		

The quantity consumed as beverage in each country in 1867-8, arrived at by adding the quantities imported from, and deducting the quantities sent to each other, and allowing for spirits warehoused on drawback for exportation and methylated, was:—England, 11,561,576 gals. ; Scotland, 4,781,390 gals. ; Ireland, 4,676,704 gals. ; total, 21,019,670 gals. Warehoused on drawback, 1,272,193 gals.; methylated, 400,490 gals. Inland Revenue Report, 1868. App. p. viii.

The high rate of the duties on spirits levied in this country was for a considerable period found to be not only a hindrance to scientific research, but a serious interference with trade, by compelling our manufacturers to resort to cheaper and inferior substitutes, which injured the character of their goods, and, in some instances, made it doubtful whether they could much longer compete with those of the Continent, where the duty on spirit is inconsiderable. In the year 1853 an artificial substitute for Sperm Oil was invented, in the manufacture of which the patentee was allowed to use spirit free of duty, the Commissioners having found, after a careful examination, that the spirit was not merely rendered unfit for drinking, but that it could not by any process be restored to its original purity. This led to further inquiries by Professors Graham, Hofmann, and Redwood, and to the preparation of methylated spirit, which, under certain restrictions, is permitted to be sold, free of duty, for manufacturing purposes. The Commissioners assert that this measure has not merely proved a direct encouragement to scientific research and manufacturing industry, but has also materially lessened the demoralizing practice of illicit distillation. It is tolerably certain that but for this relaxation it would have been impossible to maintain the spirit duties at their present high rate.*

The revenue derived from the consumption of foreign spirits amounted, in 1800, to £1,382,718, the rate of

---

* First Inland Revenue Report, 1857, pp. 6, 7, 8.

duty being 11s. 1d. per imperial gallon. In 1841, the rate having been advanced to £1 2s. 10d. per gallon, the revenue amounted to no more than £1,354,079. The sum which it should have yielded, in 1841, according to the increased rate and the additional population, was £3,840,279, being £2,465,767, or 179 per cent. in excess of the amount really collected. The following table shows the effect of excessive duties upon the consumption of legally imported spirits. Owing to the high price of corn in 1801 and 1811, distillation was prohibited in this country. The consumption of both British and foreign spirits was, therefore, exceptional, and the years 1802 and 1812 have been taken for comparison.*

Duty on foreign spirits, except rum.

	Great Britain, per gall.			Ireland, per gall.		Total consumption.
	£	s.	d.	s.	d.	Gallons.
1802	0	11	4¾	8	6	2,431,577
1812	1	4	9¼	12	7½	195,693
1821	1	2	7½	17	3¾	1,013,400
1831		£1	2 6			1,268,198
1838		1	2 6			1,232,574
1841		1	2 10			1,186,104

The diminished consumption of 1812 was caused by the war, which closed the continental ports. The high rates of duty, imposed in the first instance as a prohibition, were maintained after the close of the war for the purpose of protection to the agriculture and industry of this country. The result is apparent in

---

* Porters' "Progress of the Nation," pp. 567-8-9.

the diminished import, respecting which Mr. Porter observes that the effect of the duty "was partially counteracted through the agency of contraband traders; but," he adds, "the remedy thus applied should be considered as the substitution of a greater evil, and one for which the legislature may be held morally responsible because of the temptation which it offers for the commission of crime." In 1846 the duty on foreign spirits was reduced from 22s. 10d. to 15s.; and in 1860, in accordance with the provisions of the French treaty, it was further reduced to 10s. 5d. per gallon. The following table shows the effect of these reductions upon the importation and consumption of brandy :—*

	Imported. Gals.	Retained for Consumption. Gals.
1841	2,918,387	1,164,506
1845	1,988,210	1,058,274
1847	2,728,471	1,537,238
1851	2,930,967	1,859,273
1855	1,943,908	1,525,578
1859	4,030,175	1,305,969
1861	2,097,934	1,598,270
1865	3,122,576	2,664,289
1866	5,621,923	3,120,950
1867	4,849,832	3,183,072
1868	4,062,884	3,317,641

The increased consumption of brandy has been produced by two causes—the reduction of the duty, in 1860, from 15s. to 10s. 5d. per gallon, and a subsequent

---

* Statistical abstract, 1841 to 1855, pp. 10, 11, 13. Ibid, 1854 to 1868, pp. 24, 25, 40, 41.

reduction in price. The average price, exclusive of duty, in 1855, was 9s. 9½d.; in 1859, 6s. 11¾d.; in 1861, 9s. 1d.; in 1865, 5s. 4¾d.; in 1866, 5s. 0½d.; in 1867, 5s. 8¾d.; and in 1868, 6s. 6d. per gallon.*

Rum, being a colonial product, has invariably been admitted at a lower rate of duty than brandy and other foreign spirits, in order to carry out the protective system in relation to our colonies. The following are the rates of duty and consumption of rum for the same years as previously given in the case of foreign spirits:—†

	Great Britain. Per gallon. s. d.	Ireland. Per gallon. s. d.	Consumption. Gallons.
1802	9 0¾	5 6¼	3,310,065
1812	13 7¾	10 3½	3,775,169
1821	13 11½	12 9	2,324,315
1831	9 0	8 6	3,624,597
1838	9s. 0d.		3,135,651
1841	9s. 4d.		2,277,970

The duty on rum was reduced to 8s. 10d. per gallon, in 1846; it was further reduced, in 1847, to 8s. 7d. per gallon in England, 4s. 5d. per gallon in Scotland, and 3s. 5d. per gallon in Ireland; it was again reduced, in 1848, to 8s. 2d. per gallon in England, 4s. per gallon in Scotland, and 3s. per gallon in Ireland. It was equalised, in 1858, at 8s. 2d. per gallon, and increased, in 1860, to 10s. 2d. per gallon. The following is the quantity

---

* Statistical abstract, 1854 to 1868, pp. 36, 37. Annual statement, 1868, p. 23.
† Porters' "Progress of the Nation," p. 568.

imported and consumed in each of the years specified:—*

	Imported. Gallons.	Consumption. Gallons.
1846	3,855,464	2,683,701
1849	4,479,549	3,039,862
1859	7,078,586	3,575,139
1861	8,114,823	3,451,384
1865	6,898,599	3,697,849
1866	7,685,180	4,127,120
1867	6,845,503	4,314,778
1868	7,035,034	3,949,947

It appears from the returns for 1868, that foreign and colonial have, to a certain extent, displaced home-made spirits, the increased consumption of the former having been accompanied by a diminution in the latter. The following table shows the relative consumption per head since 1859:—†

	Foreign & Colonial. Gallons.	British & Irish. Gallons.	Total. Gallons.
1859	0·17	0·84	1·01
1861	0·18	0·68	0·86
1865	0·23	0·71	0·94
1866	0·26	0·75	1·01
1867	0·28	0·71	0·99
1868	0·28	0·70	0·98

There is no doubt whatever, that the maintenance of the excessive rate of duty on foreign spirits was productive of much smuggling. The reduction to 15s., in 1846, and to 10s. 5d., in 1860, have considerably

---

* Statistical Abstract, 1841 to 1855, pp. 10, 11, 13. Ibid, 1854 to 1868, pp. 24, 25, 40, 41.

† Statistical abstract, 1854 to 1868, pp. 42, 43.

reduced the practice by rendering it less profitable. Another cause, however, was at work. The vines of France were visited, in 1855, by a disease which diminished production and increased price. The average quantity of brandy imported annually during the six years, 1849-54, had been 3,762,728 gallons, which the increase of price reduced, during the four following years, 1855-58, to 2,112,240 gallons.* The Commissioners of Customs state, in their Report for 1859, that from the date of the failure of the wine crop in France attempts to smuggle brandy into this country appeared to have ceased, the price of the article being so high as to deprive the smuggler of his usual profit, but were recommenced in 1858.† The cases reported in subsequent years are few in number until the year 1867, when a considerable increase was recorded. The total number of gallons seized at the outports, in 1866, in quantities of two gallons and upwards, was 163; in 1867, 439; and in 1868, 460 gallons.‡ These are, however, the records of seizures: there are no statistics of the number of gallons which have been smuggled in successful ventures.

Another evil fostered, if not mainly created, by excessive duties is the practice of adulteration with deleterious compounds, which tend to provoke excessive consumption and aggravate its injurious

---

* Statistical Abstract, 1841 to 1855, p. 11. Ibid, 1854 to 1868, p. 24.
† Fourth Customs Report, 1860, p. 21.
‡ Twelfth Customs Report, 1868, p. 65. Thirteenth ditto, 1869, p. 57.

consequences. It is alleged that adulteration would be unprofitable were it not for the high duties levied by the Government. It is, therefore, a matter deserving serious enquiry whether the evils of intemperance are not aggravated rather than restrained by the imposition of a heavy tax upon the consumption of spirits. It is a well-known fact, that the arithmetic of the customs does not follow the recognised rules of the science, and it may, perhaps, be proved upon further enquiry that the Custom House is equally defective as a teacher of morality.

CHAPTER V.

WINE.

The following are the rates of duty, quantities taxed, and total gross produce for the year 1868-9:—*

	Rates of Duty.	Quantities Taxed. Gallons.	Gross Produce. £
Containing less than 26 degrees of Proof Spirit	1s. per gallon.	4,948,254	247,835
Containing 26 and less than 42 degs. of Proof Spirit	2s. 6d. per gallon.	10,197,779	1,274,363
Containing 42 or more degrees of Proof Spirit	2s. 6d. ,, and 3d. additional for each degree of strength beyond 41.	9,122	1,331
	Total	15,155,155	1,523,529

The history of Wine in this country affords a remarkable example of the way in which the taste of a nation may be perverted by the imposition of excessive duties. Mr. G. R. Porter, in his " Progress

---

* Parliamentary Paper " Taxes and Imposts." Session 1869, No. 427.

of the Nation," says :—" In former times the taste of Englishmen led them to a far greater proportionate use of French wine, but, by the ill-judged Methuen Treaty, concluded in 1703, whereby we bound ourselves to impose 50 per cent. higher duties on the wine of France than on that of Portugal, a great change in this respect was gradually brought about, so that the consumption of French wine was in time reduced to a quantity altogether insignificant."

The Methuen Treaty ceased to operate in 1831, and from that time until 1860 the same rate of duty was charged upon wine of all kinds. The following are the rates imposed per imperial gallon at different periods.*

	Great Britain.		Ireland.	
Years.	French.	Other kinds.	French.	Other kinds.
	s. d.	s. d.	s. d.	s. d.
1801	10 2½	6 9¾	6 1¼	3 11
1811	13 8½	9 1¼	10 6	7 0½
1821	13 9	9 1¼	13 9	9 1¼
1831	5 6	5 6	5 6	5 6
1841	5 6	5 6	5 6	5 6

In 1841 an additional 5 per cent. was added, which increased the duty to 5s. 9³⁄₁₀d. per gallon, at which rate it was continued till the year 1860, when it was reduced to 3s. until the 31st December. From the 1st January, 1861, the duty was reduced to 1s. per gallon on wines imported in the wood, and containing less than 18 degrees of proof spirit; 1s. 9d. less than 26 ; 2s. 5d. less than 40 ; and 2s. 11d. less than 45.

---

* Porter's " Progress of the Nation," edition, 1847, p 570.

When imported in bottle and containing less than 40 degrees of proof spirit, the duty was reduced to 2s. 5d. In 1866 the present scale was adopted, and the duties on wine imported in bottle and in the wood were equalized.* The duty on wines from the Cape and other British Possessions was for a long time fixed at a very low rate. In 1825 it was reduced from 3s. 0½d. to 2s. 5d. per gallon; in 1853 it was increased to 2s. 10⅔d. per gallon; and in 1860 it was equalized at the same rate as on foreign wines. The quantity imported from South Africa in 1859 was 786,621 gallons; in 1868 it was 12,328 gallons.†

The following table shows the quantity of wine of all kinds imported and retained for home consumption since 1854.‡

	Importation. Gallons.	Consumption. Gallons.	Per head.
1854	10,875,855	6,776,086	0·24
1855	8,946,766	6,296,439	0·23
1856	9,481,880	7,004,953	0·25
1857	10,336,845	6,601,690	0·23
1858	5,791,636	6,268,685	0·22
1859	8,195,513	6,775,992	0·24
1860	12,475,001	6,718,585	0·23
1861	11,052,436	10,693,071	0·37
1862	11,960,676	9,764,155	0·33
1863	14,185,195	10,420,761	0·35
1864	15,451,593	11,397,764	0·39
1865	14,269,752	11,993,760	0·40
1866	15,321,028	13,244,864	0·44
1867	15,442,581	13,673,793	0·45
1868	16,953,454	15,064,628	0·50

* Fifth Customs Report, 1861, p 59. Eleventh ditto, 1867, p 75.
† Customs and Excise Return, 1858, No. 511. Fifth Customs Report, 1861, p. 61. Annual Statement, 1859, p 112. Ibid, 1868, p 108.
‡ Statistical Abstract, 16th No., 1869, pp 24-25, 40-43.

The consumption during the previous ten years was almost stationary, the lowest being 6,053,847 gallons in 1847, and the highest 6,838,684 gallons in 1844.*

The following table showing the quantity of French Wine sold for home consumption and the rates of duty thereon, between 1815 and 1845, is summarised from a more elaborate statement in Porter's "Progress of the Nation."†

Years.			Average Consumption. Gallons.	Duty per gallon.	
1815	—	1818	182,408	13	8½
1819	—	1824	177,538	13	9
	1825		525,579	7	2¼
1826	—	1830	350,019	7	3
1831	—	1835	249,566		
1836	—	1840	389,600	5	6
1841	—	1845	396,744		

A Memorandum on the Commercial relations between France and England, printed at the Foreign Office in 1853, gives the following statistics of the quantity of French Wine imported in each of the three specified years :—

	Imported Gallons.	Consumed Gallons.
1831	335,430	266,113
1841	462,515	363,559
1851	750,204	456,489

The following table shows the quantities of French

---

* Statistical Abstract, 1856, p 13.
† Edit. 1847. p 571.

Wines imported and consumed in each year since 1858.*

	Gallons.	Gallons.
1858	623,041	571,993
1859	1,010,888	695,913
1860	2,445,151	1,125,916
1861	2,187,521	2,229,028
1862	2,244,727	1,901,200
1863	2,186,706	1,940,193
1864	2,723,233	2,305,756
1865	2,915,357	2,611,771
1866	3,668,812	3,366,073
1867	3,771,301	3,595,598
1868	4,745,440	4,502,162

It is quite clear from these facts that the excessive duties imposed upon the light wines of France were to a very large extent prohibitory of their use, and that the fiscal policy of the government developed a taste for the stronger and, in many instances, brandied wines of Spain and Portugal. The reductions of duty effected in 1860 and 1866 have been productive of very remarkable results in changing the direction of the public taste. It would be unreasonable to expect that the work of more than half a century should be reversed in a few years. Comparison, however, of the year 1858 with the year 1868 shows that considerable progress has been made.†

Consumption of Wine.	1858. Gallons	1868. Gallons.	Increase per cent.
From Spain	2,657,131	6,182,904	132½
,, Portugal	1,921,677	2,853,612	48
,, France	571,993	4,502,162	687

---

* Annual Statements of Trade and Navigation, 1858—1868.
† Annual Statements, 1858, 1859.

The marked increase in the consumption of French wines has created a controversy on the wine duties. Negociations were commenced in 1866 between the Portuguese and the British Governments for a Commercial Treaty, Portugal binding herself to a reduction on some British manufactures, if our Government would reduce the duty on Portuguese wines of 40 degrees and under to a shilling per gallon. To this the Revenue Authorities object on the ground that wines would be imported for the purpose of distillation, and the spirit revenue would be endangered. In reply, it is asserted that the cost of producing spirits from wine would render the transaction unprofitable, and that it could not be carried on to any extent without the knowledge of the revenue authorities. If the present plan of taxing the alcohol in beer, wine, and spirits is maintained, the equalisation of the duties is not practicable. If a change is made it will become necessary to revise the entire scale of duties upon Alcoholic beverages. An increased import of wines from Portugal would, no doubt, be followed by an increase in our exports to that country. The wine question is analogous to that of the sugar duties. In the one case, it is attempted to tax the saccharine matter in sugar, in the other to tax the alcohol in wine. In neither case does the process appear to give universal satisfaction.

CHAPTER VI.

SUGAR AND ARTICLES OF WHICH SUGAR IS AN INGREDIENT.

A Parliamentary paper issued in 1857 respecting the consumption of tea and sugar, and containing very copious returns of consumption by the various classes of the community, says that "the consumption of tea and sugar among the working and poorer classes has steadily and gradually increased to such an extent, that these articles have now become, next to bread, the prime necessaries of life." Mr. Dudley Baxter, in his work on Taxation, gives the result of his enquiries in every part of the United Kingdom, in the following words:—"Irish families in Connemara, who seldom taste meat, are great consumers of tea and sugar, eating the sugar upon their bread and in their stir-about in large quantities as often as they can get it. The underpaid and highly-rented poor at the East-end of London depend almost as much upon the same articles."* A tax on sugar is emphatically a tax upon one of the prime necessaries of life, and upon an important article of commerce.

---

* Taxation of the United Kingdom, pp. 77—78.

The history of the sugar trade is a remarkable illustration of the prejudicial effects of protective duties and high customs tariffs. Until the year 1847 it was the avowed object of the Government to exclude foreign, and especially slave-grown sugar, from the English market. Consumers of slave-grown cotton and tobacco were scandalised at the idea of using slave-grown sugar; to the former they submitted without a murmur, but the bare possibility of the latter aroused their righteous indignation, and called forth loud remonstrances. The reason for much of this indignation was obvious; the West Indian planters, who had received £20,000,000 compensation upon the abolition of their legal right to hold property in man, required a further and perpetual compensation from their long patient friend the British taxpayer, in the shape of a protective duty upon their produce. Their protests were, however, unavailing, and they were told that, like the British landlords, they must endeavour to walk without crutches.

The rates of duty levied upon raw sugar, in 1830, were as follows:—

British West India and Mauritius -	£1 4 0	per cwt.
East India - - - - -	1 12 0	,,
Foreign - - - - - -	3 3 0	,,

In 1836 an additional distinction was introduced, the duty on sugar "of any British possession within the limits of the East India's Company's charter, into which the importation of foreign sugar is prohibited, and imported from thence," being reduced to £1 4s., the duty of £1 12s. being retained upon sugar from other British possessions in the East Indies. In 1840 an additional 5 per cent. was added to all the duties; and in 1844 a further classification of foreign sugar was introduced, the duty on such sugar, not being the produce of slave labour, being reduced to £1 15s. 8$\frac{9}{50}$d. In 1845 the duties were considerably reduced, with the exception of slave grown sugar, the rate of which was fixed at £3 3s. In 1846 the distinction between free and slave grown sugar was abolished, and a gradual reduction of duties, year by year, was commenced, which terminated, in 1854, by the equalization of the duties upon sugar irrespective of its place of production.*

Under the influence of the protective system, the consumption of sugar was considerably diminished. During the fourteen years ending 1841 it averaged 18lb. 7oz. per head of the population; during the fourteen years ending 1844 it averaged only 17lb. 2oz.; the reduction and equalization of the duties increased the consumption to 34lbs. per head in 1854. In 1855 additional duties were imposed in consequence of the Crimean War, and the average rate of duty on raw sugar being increased from 12s. 4d. to 15s. 5d. per cwt., the consumption fell to 28lbs. per head; in consequence of subsequent reductions, it again increased, and in 1868 the consumption of raw sugar was 39·56lbs. per head.†

---

* Tea and Sugar Return. Sess. 1857. No. 184.

† Tea and Sugar Return. Sess. 1857, No. 184. Statistical Abstract, 1869, p. 43.

The following table shows the alterations made since 1854, and the quantity of each description taxed, and the amount produced during the year 1868–9 :—*

CUSTOMS.	1854. Per cwt. s. d.	1855. Per cwt. s. d.	1857. Per cwt. s. d.	1864. Per Cwt. s. d.	1867. Per Cwt. s. d.	Quantities Taxed. Cwt.	Amount Produced. £
Refined & candy	16 0	20 0	18 4	12 10	12 0	773,789	464,174
1st class, equal to white clayed	14 0	17 6	16 0	11 8	11 3	65,575	36,890
2nd class, not equal to white clayed, but equal to brown clayed	12 0	15 0	13 10	10 6	10 6	3,006,101	1,578,489
3rd class, not equal to brown clayed, but equal to brown muscovado	11 0	13 9	12 8	9 4	9 7	3,766,564	1,805,188
4th class, not equal to brown muscovado, including cane juice	Sugar, same rate as 3rd class before 1864. Cane juice, 10s. 4d.			8 2	8 0	4,325,943	1,730,643
Molasses	4 3	5 4	5 0	3 6	3 6	840,227	118,041
Glucose (liquid) or vegetable spirit	Increased in 1865, to 8s. 2d.			6 7	According to the quantity of saccharine matter.	13,726	4,882
							£5,738,307

The effect upon consumption of these changes is shown in the the following table :—†

---

* Acts 17 & 18 Vic. c. 29. 18 Vic. c. 21. 20 & 21 Vic. c. 61. Ninth Customs Report 1865, p. 55. Twelfth ditto. 1868, p. 83. Parliamentary Paper "Taxes and Imposts," Sess. 1869. No. 427.

† Statistical Abstract 1869, pp. 86—43. Annual Statement 1868, p. 23.

Year.	Quantity of Raw Sugar entered for Home Consumption. Cwts.	Per Head. lbs.	Average price per cwt. of Yellow Muscovado or Brown-clayed Sugar.	
			Cuba. s. d.	Brit. West Indies s. d.
1854	8,028,758	32·51	22 9	22 6
1855	7,259,148	29·22	26 6	27 4
1856	6,813,470	27·24	31 0	31 0
1857	7,121,590	28·30	38 0	39 6
1858	8,490,256	33·50	30 9	30 1
1859	8,641,920	33·85	29 5	28 3
1860	8,506,882	33·11	29 7	28 10
1861	8,937,302	34·55	24 9	25 0
1862	9,111,621	34·94	22 9	23 4
1863	9,202,523	35·06	22 0	22 11
1864	8,937,313	33·86	27 10	29 1
1865	9,878,933	37·17	22 10	22 5
1866	10,297,196	38·53	21 5	22 0
1867	10,925,793	40·58	22 0	24 1
1868	10,729,601	39·56	24 0	24 3

The diminished consumption of 1855, 1856, and 1857, as compared with 1854, is attributed by the customs authorities more to the advance in price of sugars in bond than to the increased rate of duty. It was, however, a misfortune that additional taxation upon sugar was considered necessary at a time when, from natural causes, there was a check placed upon consumption. It could have but one effect, that of further limiting the demand. According to a report of the Surveyor-General of the Customs, the increased duty obtained was only 2 per cent., although the rate of duties had

---

* First Customs Report, 1857, pp. 49—50, 116.

been advanced 25 per cent.:* a rather unprofitable speculation from a commercial point of view. It was not until the year 1858, that the consumption of 1854 was again reached. Nor was it materially increased until the year 1865, when the combined effects of a reduction in the duty and in the price, as compared with 1858, of 7s. 11d. per cwt., or a trifle more than ¾d. per lb., increased the consumption to 37·17 per head.

The history of the increased duties levied on sugar, in consequence of the Crimean War, affords an admirable illustration of the mode by which such taxes enable the Government to extract a revenue from the pockets of unwilling contributors. By the act imposing them† a gradual reduction was provided for in the following manner:—

	Until April 5, after the Peace. per cwt. £ s. d.	Succeeding Twelve Months. per cwt. s. d.	Thereafter. per cwt. s. d.
Refined and Candy	1 0 0	16 8	13 4
1st Class	0 17 6	14 7	11 8
2nd Class	0 15 0	12 9	10 6
3rd Class	0 13 9	11 8	9 6
Molasses	0 5 4	4 6	3 9

The Treaty of Peace was signed on the 30th March, 1856, but the war duties on sugar, which ought to have expired in 1857, on the 5th of April following the exchange of ratifications, were not finally repealed until the year 1864. The war income tax, however, was remitted one year sooner than the date fixed by

---

* First Customs Report, 1857, p.p. 49—50, 116.
† 18 Vic. c. 21

the Act of Parliament by which it was imposed. The different treatment of the two burdens, and the violation of the stipulations under which they were both imposed may perhaps be explained by the fact that, at that time, payers of income tax enjoyed an exclusive predominance in our electoral system. It was none the less unjust as regarded the unrepresented consumers of sugar, upon whom it imposed a heavy burden of seven years' duration.

The imposition of a tax upon this necessary of life involves the additional evil of a duty on each of the following articles, in the composition of which sugar is an ingredient:—*

	Rate of duty 1d. per lb.	Quantities Taxed lbs.	Gross Amount Produced in 1868-9.
Almond Paste		102	—
Cherries, dried		283	1
Comfits, dry		—	—
Confectionery		363,778	1,516
Ginger, preserved		321,561	1,340
Marmalade		17,942	75
Plums, preserved in Sugar		482	2
Succades		526,219	2,193
Total			£5,127

	Rate of Duty. Various.	cwts.	
Excise.			
Sugar, Home Made	8s. to 12s. per cwt.	17,443	7,180
Used by Brewers	2s. 6d.	369,350	64,636
Customs Duties from page 40		…	5,738,307
Total of Duty received on Sugar and Articles containing Sugar			£5,815,250

---

* Parliamentary Paper, Session 1869, No. 427.

The sugar duties have been productive of a controversy between grocers and refiners, which it would occupy a volume of considerable size to discuss fully. The former advocate one uniform duty; the latter maintain the principle of a graduated scale. Both grocers and refiners rest their advocacy upon the principles of Free Trade as commonly understood, viz., that no advantage should be afforded by our fiscal policy to either home, colonial, or foreign producers, manufacturers, or dealers. The present scale of duties has been framed with the intention of securing this result, by taxing every description of sugar according to the quantity of saccharine matter it contains. It is advocated by the refiners and has been supported by the high authority of Mr. Gladstone, and the late Richard Cobden. The grocers, on the other hand, and in their contention they have been supported by many eminent sugar merchants, maintain that a uniform duty, accompanied by the privilege of refining in bond, would be at once the most advantageous mode of raising a revenue from sugar, and a sufficient safeguard of the interests of the refiners. The Chairman and Inspector-General of Customs were examined, as to the proposal to allow refining in bond, before a Parliamentary Committee in 1862, and they both expressed a decided opinion that it would be impossible to protect the revenue if the practice were allowed.

The advocates of a uniform duty urge that the existing system of discriminating duties forbids the planters to make fine sugar, rewards the indolent, and ruins the diligent; that 3,000,000 tons are produced annually, but that the plants which produce them contain 6,000,000 tons at least, and that thus a quantity of sugar equal to that now produced, and worth £60,000,000 in bond, is directly sacrificed in consequence of the slothful manufacture fostered by the graduated duties. It is also alleged that two-thirds of the sugar produced is exported in a damp state, and unfit for consumption, in order to secure admission at a low rate of duty, and that in consequence there is a drainage of 15 per cent., representing a loss of 300,000 tons on the voyage. That the cost of refining this sugar is excessive, and that the combined effect of these evils is to double the price of sugar, independently of the duty imposed upon it.* If these statements are correct, and if, as asserted upon the same authority, the price of sugar would be reduced two-thirds by its admission free of duty, it is clear that a good case has been made out for the entire repeal of the sugar duties at the earliest practicable period.

A practical illustration of the effect of a graduated scale of duties in preventing the sale of the best qualities of raw sugar was afforded the author some years since in Newcastle-on-Tyne. He was shown a sample of East-India raw sugar, which, owing to its assessment at the highest rate of duty, was not marketable in this country. Not being loaf sugar, purchasers could not understand the reason of its excessive price as compared with other raw sugars, and the

---

* Produce Markets Review, December 5, 1868.

consequence was that its consumption was confined to foreign seagoing ships, which are supplied with their stores free of duty.

Another instance of the vexatious interference with trade to which such duties always give rise has recently occurred. A sugar has been brought out, intended not merely as a dietetic article of consumption, but possessing, as averred by Dr. Watson Bradshaw (a well-known authority on dietetics, dyspepsia, and diseases of the digestive organs), undoubted medicinal virtues, inasmuch as it is a sugar which invalids and dyspeptics may take, when ordinary cane sugar is altogether inadmissible. It is also asserted, on the same authority, that it is pre-eminently adapted for consumption by infants in lieu of ordinary sugar. In applying for a patent considerable difficulty was experienced at the hands of the Excise, and ultimately the rate of duty payable upon it was fixed at £12 per ton, the highest rate in the scale. The dietetic properties of this sugar entitle it to rank more as a remedial agent than as a substance possessing only dulcifying properties. It is called by the proprietor, Mr. Alexander Manbre, Dietetic Grape Sugar; it is prepared pound for pound from sago or tapioca; and its invention is considered, by many who are competent to judge, to be a triumph of Modern Chemistry. It opens an entirely new supply of sugar for the consumer, of a very superior quality, the consumption of which will necessarily be limited by the high rate of duty imposed.

The following table shows the total quantity of sugar and molasses imported and consumed in 1844, 1854, 1864 and 1868.*

	Imported cwts.	Consumed cwts.
1844	5,502,849	4,129,449†
1854	10,541,050	9,259,673
1864	12,279,620	10,239,981
1868	13,372,490	12,220,004

During the seven years ending 1867, our imports of sugar came in about equal proportions from Foreign Countries and our Colonial Possessions. If by improved processes of production, consequent upon the entire relief of this article from taxation, the production of sugar in our Colonies could be doubled, it is evident that the prosperity of those portions of the Empire would be greatly promoted; in return for our increased imports of sugar there would also be a corresponding increase in the demand for British manufactures.

There are other aspects of the sugar duty as it affects trade and manufactures, not less important than those already noticed. The argument recently used respecting corn, that the removal of the duty would make this country the depôt of Europe, applies with even greater force to sugar. It is well known that trade loves freedom; wherever there are the fewest restrictions, capital and employment locate themselves in the

---

* Statistical Abstract, 1856, pp. 10, 11, 13.   Ibid, 1869, pp. 24-25, 40-41.
† The consumption of 1844 does not include Molasses.

greatest abundance. Were sugar admitted into Great Britain and Ireland duty free, there is little doubt that these islands would become the sugar market of Europe. There is no reason whatever why sugar should not become as important a feature in our export trade as tea, coffee, cotton, or wool. The one thing necessary to secure this result, in the case of sugar, is by entirely repealing the heavy tax of nearly 40 per cent. now levied upon that article. There is another valid objection to this duty; it is mainly a tax upon a raw material. The records of our imports of sugar prove this fact, inasmuch as the importation of refined sugar, and of sugar equal in quality thereto, in the year 1868, was only 729,865 cwts., while that of raw sugar was 11,796,161 cwts., and has been invariably 10,000,000 cwts. in excess of refined during the last five years.* Sugar is also extensively used in the manufacture of confectionery of various kinds, a branch of industry which would be vastly increased were the raw material to be obtained free of duty. At present this trade is in a languid state, an evil which the removal of the tax would effectually remedy. Many manufacturers of confectionery have removed their manufactures from Great Britain to the Channel Islands and elsewhere, where lower duties are imposed upon sugar. In relation to agriculture, especially in Ireland, the question is also one of vital importance. The manufacture of

---

* Annual Statement, 1868, p. 16.

beet root sugar would introduce a profitable article of cultivation, for which many parts of the sister island are admirably adapted.

To sum up the arguments against this tax; it is levied upon an article of universal consumption and a prime necessary of life; it is imposed not upon sugar fit for the table, but upon the raw material before it passes into the hands of the refiner; it places serious restrictions upon our home trade and manufactures, and retards the development of colonial industry; it lays a burden upon the taxpayer out of all proportion to the amount which it brings into the treasury. In all these respects it offends against the canons of taxation laid down by Adam Smith, and now recognised by all authorities on the subject. Its removal would be a boon to all classes of the community, and would stimulate trade and industry in every part of the United Kingdom.

CHAPTER VII.

TEA.

The consumption of tea was for a long period held in check in this country, notwithstanding the fact that a taste for it had been diffused among all classes, by two causes; the high price consequent upon its importation being a monopoly of the East India Company, and the excessive duty levied upon it by the Government. The following were the rates of duty from the commencement of the present century to the year 1852:—*

	Per cent. ad valorem.	
	If sold at or above 2s. 6d. per lb. £ s. d.	If sold under 2s. 6d. per lb. £ s. d.
1801—1802	50 0 0	20 0 0
1803—1804	95 0 0	65 0 0
1805	95 2 6	65 2 6
1806—1818	£96	

	If sold at or above 2s. per lb.	If sold at or under 2s. per lb.
1819—1833	£100	£96

	Bohea. per lb.	Congou, Twankay, Hyson Skin, Orange Pekoe, and Campoi. per lb.	Other sorts. per lb.
1834	1s. 6d.	2s. 2d.	3s.
			On all sorts. s. d.
1836			2 1
1840—1852			2 2¼

* Parliamentary Paper, Tea and Sugar, Session 1857, No. 184, p. 9.

The annual consumption per head from 1801 to 1833, when the East India Company enjoyed their monopoly, varied from 1 lb. 3 oz. to 1 lb. 9 oz. per head. The average of the five years, 1801-1805, was not quite 1 lb. 8 oz. per head; during the five years, 1829-1833, it was 1 lb. 4 oz. per head; showing a decrease of 4 oz. In the year 1834 the trade was thrown open, and from that period the consumption has gradually increased, so that in 1852 it reached 2 lbs. per head.*

The following table shows the various modifications of the duty since that period, and their effect upon importation and consumption :—†

Year.	Duty per ℔.	Total imported. ℔.	Consumption. Per ℔.	Per head. ℔.
	s. d.			
1852	2 2¼	66,360,535	54,713,034	2
1853	1 10	70,735,135	58,834,087	2·14
1854	1 6	85,792,032	61,953,041	2·24
1855	1 9	83,259,657	63,429,286	2·28
1856	1 9	86,200,414	63,278,212	2 26
1857	1 5	64,493,989	69,132,101	2·45
1862	1 5	114,787,361	78,793,977	2·70
1863	1 0	136,806,321	85,183,280	2·90
1864	1 0	124,359,243	88,599,235	3·00
1865	0 6	121,271,219	97,834,600	3 29
1866	0 6	139,610,044	102,265,531	3·42
1867	0 6	128,028,726	110,988,209	3·68
1868	0 6	154,815,863	106,815,311	3 52

The amount of revenue for the year 1868-9 was

---

* Parliamentary Paper, Tea and Sugar, Sess. 1857, No. 184, p. 8.
† Statistical Abstract, 1856, pp. 11, 13. Parliamentary Paper, Session 1857, No. 184. Statistical Abstract, 1869, pp. 24, 25, 40, 43.

£2,597,980. Originally a luxury of the rich, tea has become a necessary of life to all classes. It has been already shown that in a Parliamentary paper issued in 1857, it was described as, next to bread, one of the prime necessaries of life. Enquiries made during the last few months by Mr. Dudley Baxter, in connection with his recent work on Taxation, show that with working people tea and coffee are more articles of food than with those who have plenty of food without them. "They drink them," he says, "three times a day—for breakfast, dinner, and tea, though weaker than we should be satisfied with." The fact that this article has given its name to one of the three recognised meals of the bulk of the population, shows its popularity. The main argument advanced in favour of taxing spirits cannot be applicable to tea. If it be right to limit the consumption of the one, it ought surely to be the duty of the Government to remove all fiscal hindrances from the increased consumption of the other. According to the statistical abstract the average price of tea from China has varied during the last fifteen years from 1s. 3d. to 1s. 8d. per lb., from India from 1s. 3d. to 2s. 4d., and from Japan from 1s. 4d. to 1s. 7d. The pressure of the duty is much heavier upon the lower class of teas than it is upon the higher, and one of its consequent disadvantages is the discouragement thus given to the importation of first-class teas. The uniform duty practically operates as a protection in favour of inferior teas. It was considered last year a wise policy to abolish the tea license, so as to allow the sale of tea in villages; would it not be far wiser to abolish the duty, and thus increase the consumption of this mild and grateful stimulant?

In addition to the effect of previous reductions of duty in increasing the consumption of tea, there has been a large increase in the exports of British Produce and Manufactures to China as a consequence of our increased imports from that country. The value of these exports to China and Hong Kong in 1852 was £2,503,599, in 1857 it was only £2,449,982, but in 1868 it reached the sum of £8,498,966.* There has also been a great increase since the reduction of the duty in the quantity of tea exported from this country. The following table shows the excess of importation over consumption and the quantities exported in each of the specified years. In 1857, owing to the War with China the consumption exceeded the importation by 4,638,112 lbs.

Year	Duty per lb.	Excess of Imports over Consumption. lbs.	Quantity Exported.* lbs.
1852	2 2¼	11,647,501	6,134,743
1853	1 11¼	11,901,048	4,836,009
1854	1 6½	23,838,991	8,655,955
1855	1 8	19,830,371	13,626,507
1856	1 9	24,922,202	5,718,764
1862	1 5	35,993,384	27,342,603
1863	1 0	51,623,041	26,219,654
1864	1 0	35,760,008	27,515,341
1865	0 6	23,436,619	32,633,151
1866	0 6	37,314,513	30,215,454
1867	0 6	17,040,517	31,131,112
1868	0 6	48,030,552	34,631,678

* Statistical Abstract 1856, p. 19.   Ibid. 1869, pp. 54-55.
* Statistical Abstract 1856, p. 23.   Ibid 1869, pp. 74, 75.

It is tolerably certain that two results would follow the repeal of the duty; an increased export of British Manufactures to China and other tea growing countries, and an augmented export trade in the article itself consequent upon the increased quantity which the demand arising from the entire repeal of the duty would attract to our shores. If the hindrances to trade which are the invariable result of Customs duties were removed, there exists no reason whatever why Great Britain should not become the tea depot of the whole of Europe, thus creating in this one article alone a considerable extension of trade, commerce, and employment, and adding to the social and domestic comforts of our population.

CHAPTER VIII.

COFFEE AND CHICORY.

These articles are now almost as inseparably united as the celebrated Siamese Twins; no apology is needed, therefore, for considering them under one and the same head. In fact a review of the one duty would be incomplete and unsatisfactory if no reference were made to the other. Mr. Porter remarks very truly in his invaluable work, that* "the facts exhibited by the history of the home or consumption trade in this article (coffee) are pregnant with lessons of great value as regards taxation. There are but few articles fitted for general use which have been subjected in an equal degree to alternations of high and low duties, and with respect to which we are consequently enabled, with equal certainty, to trace the effects of taxation in contracting or enlarging the enjoyments of the people, or to mark the comparative advantage thus produced to the Exchequer.

The following table of the duties levied at various periods taken from a Parliamentary Paper† issued in 1857 is very interesting, and affords an admirable example of the mode in which the people of this country were formerly taxed for the benefit of individuals by the protective system so long established.

---

* Progress of the Nation. 1847. p. 558.

† Tea and Sugar. Session 1857. No. 184, p. 11. The fractional parts of a penny in the years 1840-44, represent the extra 5 per cent. imposed in 1840.

Duties levied upon Coffee, 1801-55:

Years.	British Possessions in America. per lb. s.	d.	East India. per lb. s.	d.		Per cent. ad val. £	s.	d.	Foreign. per lb. s.	d.
1801	1	5 1/2	2	7	and	2	0	0	2	7
1802	1	6	2	7 1/2	,,	2	0	0	2	7 1/2
1803	1	6 3/4	1	11 5/8	,,	2	16	3	2	5 3/4
1804	1	7 1/4	2	0 1/4	,,	3	2	6	2	6 1/4
1805	2	1 1/2	2	6 3/8	,,	3	3	9	3	0 1/2
1806-7	2	1 7/8	2	6 3/4	,,	3	7	11	3	0 7/8
1808	0	7	0	10	,,	3	7	11	2	4
1809-12	0	7	0	10	,,	3	6	8	2	4
1813	0	7 3/4	0	10 3/4	,,	3	19	2	2	4 3/4
			Per lb.							
1814-18	0	7 3/4	0	11 1/2					2	4 3/4
1819-24	1	0	1	6					2	6
1825	0	6	0	9					1	3

	Of and from British Possessions in America. Per lb.	Imported from places within the limits of the East India Company's Charter. British Possessions. per lb.		Imported from places within the limits of the East India Company's Charter. Other places. per lb.	Otherwise Imported. per lb.
1826-1834	6d.	9d.		1s.	1s. 3d.
		Certified as produce of British Possns. per lb.	Not Certified as produce of British Possns. per lb.		
1835-1839	6d.	6d.	9d.	1s.	1s. 3d.
1840-1841	6 3/10	6 3/10d.	9 3/10d.	1s. 6/10d.	1s. 3 3/4d.

		Of and from British Possessions. per lb.		Of and from Foreign Countries. per lb.
1842—from 9th July	...	4 1/5d.	...	8 2/5d.
1844—from 6th June	...	4 1/5d.	...	6 3/10d.

Of whatever Growth and whencesoever Imported.

				per lb.
1845—from 15th April ...	..	...	...	4d.
1855—from 21st April ...	...	...	...	3d.

The extra penny imposed in 1855 to meet a portion of the cost of the Crimean War was removed in 1857, since which period the duty has remained at 3d. per lb. The rates of duty, quantities taxed, and amount collected in 1868-9 were as follows :—*

	lbs.	£
Raw, 3d. per lb.	28,557,200	356,976
Kiln dried, roasted, or ground, 4d. per lb.	3,668	61
		£357,037

The following tables show the alterations in the duty and their effect upon consumption, imports, and exports of foreign and colonial coffee since 1841 :—†

Year.	Rate of Duty.		Consumption.		Total.
	Foreign, per lb.	Colonial, per lb.	Foreign. lbs.	Colonial. lbs.	
1841	see above		10,838,409	17,532,448	28,370,857
1842	8	4	11,219,646	17,299,916	28,519,646
1843	8	4	9,848,774	20,130.630	29,979,404
1844	6	4	11,815,758	19,536,624	31,352,382
1850	6	4	2,316,323	28,850,035	31,166,358
1851	3	3	4,563,830	27,940,715	32,504,545
1854	3	3	6,542,698	30,808,226	37,350,924
1855	4	4	6,370,508	29,394,056	35,764,564
1857	3	3	6,995,334	27,357,789	34,353,123
1867	3	3	5,298,513	25,983,510	31,282,023
1868	3	3	4,804,304	25,552,741	30,357,045

It appears that in 1841, under the protective system, more than 60 per cent. of the coffee consumed in this country was of foreign production; while in 1868 the proportion of foreign to colonial was, in round numbers, 18 per cent.

---

* Parliamentary Paper, Taxes and Imposts, Session 1869, No. 427.

† Statistical Abstract, 1841 to 1855, pp. 8, 9, 13, 22, 23. Ibid, 1854 to 1868, pp. 20, 21, 40, 41, 72, 73.

	Imports.		Exports.	
Year.	Foreign. lbs.	Colonial. lbs.	Foreign. lbs.	Colonial. lbs.
1841	26,256,770	17,060,992	13,914,254	359,842
1851	17,138,497	35,972,163	10,106,276	12,606,583
1857	18,280,672	40,612,054	4,055,856	11,726,854
1867	33,937,404	103,792,312	26,139,824	71,456,123
1868	37,681,327	136,221,150	31,861,106	103,205,228
Increase of 1868 over 1841	11,424,557	119,160,158	17,946,852	102,845,386

It is shown clearly by these returns that the effort to stimulate the trade in colonial coffee by means of protective duties was a complete failure, and that the abolition of that pernicious policy was a boon to our colonial possessions as far as coffee is concerned.

The average consumption per head during the present century is shown in the following table :—*

Period of 4 Years.	lbs.	oz.	Single Years.	lbs.
1801—1804		1	1856	1·25
Periods of 5 Years.			1857	1·22
1805—1809		3	1858	1·24
1810—1814		6	1859	1·20
1815—1819		6	1860	1·23
1820—1824		6	1861	1·21
1825—1829		11	1862	1·18
1830—1834		15	1863	1·11
1835—1839	1	0	1864	1·06
1840—1844	1	1	1865	1·02
1845—1849	1	5	1866	1·02
1850—1854	1	4	1867	1·04
Single Years.			1868	1·00
1855	1	4		
1856	1	4		

* Parliamentary Paper, Tea and Sugar, Sess., 1857, No. 184, p. 10. Statistical Abstract, 1854 to 1868, pp. 42, 43.

The statistics of the consumption of coffee afford an admirable illustration of the effect of duties of customs and excise in developing the practice of adulteration. By the Act 43, Geo. III., cap. 129, the manufacturing or selling of any vegetable substance so as to resemble or serve as a substitute for coffee was prohibited. Notwithstanding this enactment, chicory, upon which the customs duty was smaller than on coffee, was extensively used for that purpose. In the year 1832, the treasury prohibited dealers from keeping for sale coffee mixed with chicory, but permitted the sale of chicory unmixed with coffee. The practice of mixing, however, was continued, and, at length, in consequence of its being found impossible to prevent this form of adulteration, it was ordered by the Treasury, in 1840, that no notice should be taken of offences against the statute; and from that date to the year 1852, when another change took place, but little pure coffee, in a ground state, was sold. The sale of the mixture was again prohibited in that year, but that of substances prepared to resemble coffee was allowed, if sold unmixed with that article. This arrangement lasted until 1853, when the sale of mixtures of chicory and coffee was legalised, provided the packages were labelled as such.* In 1861 the Inland Revenue Commissioners† attributed the diminished consumption of coffee mainly to its adulteration with chicory, and asserted that in the case of coffee purchased at 1s. 4 1.

---

* First Inland Revenue Report, 1857, Appendix, pp. 15, 16.
† Fifth Inland Revenue Report, 1861, Appendix, pp. 19, 20.

per lb., there was no limit to the proportion of the latter article introduced; it was found, in some instances, that such samples were composed entirely of chicory. The following table giving the average results of analysis made in the laboratory department accompanies these observations:—

Years.	Pure Coffee.	Average per centage of Chicory found in samples purchased as Mixtures of Coffee and Chicory.
1856	21·3	25·8
1857	22·2	26·7
1858	26·8	30·7
1859	24·2	39·8
1860	29·1	39·3

Numerous alterations have been made in the customs duty on chicory since 1832.* In that year it was increased from 20 per cent. *ad valorem* to 6d. per lb. In 1836 it was reduced on raw chicory to 20s., and on roasted or ground to £2 16s. per cwt. In 1842 raw or kiln dried was charged £10 per cwt. if from foreign countries, and 20s. per cwt. from British possessions; roasted or ground, of all kinds, 6d. per lb. In 1845 the duty on foreign raw and kiln dried, was reduced to the same rate as that charged on chicory from British possessions. In 1853 it was reduced to 4s. per cwt., and in 1854 was entirely repealed. During the above period no excise duty was levied on home grown chicory.

---

* Parliamentary Paper, "Customs and Excise," Session 1858, No. 511, p. 19. Acts of Parliament 3 and 4 Wm. IV., c. 56. 5 and 6 Vic. c., 47. 8 Vic., c. 12 16 and 17 Vic., c. 54.

The loss to the revenue caused by the extensive adulteration of coffee which resulted from the free admission of foreign and colonial, and the absence of any excise upon home grown, chicory led, in the year 1860, to the imposition of duties, both of customs and excise. It will be seen from the following analysis, compiled from the Annual Reports of the Commissioners of Customs and Inland Revenue, of the rates of duty levied since 1860, that an effort has been made to remove all inducement to defraud the revenue by the substitution, in whole or in part, of an untaxed commodity for one upon which a duty is levied varying from 30 to 50 per cent.*

Rates of Duty on Chicory.

	Customs. per cwt. s. d.	Excise. per cwt. s. d.
1860	6 0	3 0
1861	12 0	6 0
1862	12 0	11 0
1863	26 6	21 9
1864-68	26 6	24 3

The effect of the duty imposed in 1860 was felt immediately, the imports declined from 127,553 cwts. in 1858,† and 266,909 cwts. in 1859† to 94,287 cwts. in 1860,† 72,363 cwts. in 1861,‡ and 45,563 cwts. in 1862;‡ in 1863‡ there was a recovery, the quantity being 131,628 cwts.; and in 1864,‡ it was further increased, being 136,272 cwts. The quantity grown

---

* Customs Reports, 1861, p. 66. 1862, p. 46. 1864, p. 53. Inland Revenue Report, 1865, App. p. 3.

† Fifth Customs Report, 1861, p. 74.

‡ Annual Statement for 1864, p. 14.

at home appears to be very small; formerly many thousands of acres were cultivated with chicory, it appears however from enquiries made in 1860 that not more than 500 acres were then under cultivation in the United Kingdom.* The following table shows the extent to which chicory is at present used.†

	Rate of Duty Per Cwt. s. d.	Quantity Taxed. 1868-9. Per Cwt.	Gross Sum Produced. 1868-9. £.
Customs:—			
Raw or Kiln dried...	26 6	77,433	102,600
Ditto produce of Channel Islands ..	24 3	1,145	1,389
Roasted or Ground	4 per lb.	3,134 lbs.	52
Excise	24 3	11,842	4,358
			£108,399

An enquiry made by the Author in June, 1869, of one of the principal wholesale coffee dealers in London as to the relative prices of chicory and coffee, and their effect upon the practice of adulteration, was answered as follows:—" the price of Raw Chicory in Bond is about £15 per ton, while coffee in bond ranges from £50 to £140 at the present time. The bulk of the consumption in England is at present about £70 to £80 per ton. There can be no question that the original use of Chicory was induced by the fact that there was no duty upon it, while there was a heavy duty on Coffee, although the duty on both is now £28 and ¼ per cent per ton. A large section of the public

---

* Mr. Gladstone's Financial Statements, 1863, p. 164.

† Parliamentary Paper Sess. 1869. No. 427.

still insists on Chicory being mixed with the Coffee, as it makes it darker and gives a somewhat more pungent taste, though of course not the proper Coffee flavour. We may fairly state that the public taste has been spoiled by the effect of the duty." The latter portion of this statement is confirmed by information communicated to the Author some years since by a retail grocer, who was recommended, by a friend in the same trade, to mix chicory with his coffee in order to meet the competition of his neighbours. At first it was disliked, in fact he used too much chicory. Subsequently he commenced with a small quantity which he gradually increased, and finally educated his customers to the standard he had originally adopted.

The injurious effects of heavy protective duties upon the interests of the Colonial growers, for whose supposed advantage they were long maintained, is shown very clearly by the history of the coffee trade. It will be seen, from the figures previously quoted, that during the era of protective duties the export trade of this country in coffee was almost monopolised by the foreign producer. The loss of protection was a gain to the Colonist, and has placed him far ahead of his Foreign competitors.

The consumption of coffee has long been stationary in this country; the amount of duty it produces is comparatively trifling; it may therefore be reasonably hoped that an early revision of the customs tariff will afford the opportunity of repealing a duty, which certainly belongs to that class of fiscal imposts—which, in 1840, were well described as " nothing but burdens, restrictions, and delays upon the industry and the prosperity of the country "

CHAPTER IX.

MINOR ARTICLES.—COCOA

This duty is maintained because tea and coffee are taxed. It is thoroughly insignificant in itself, and can only be defended upon the very improbable theory that people would forsake tea and coffee and drink cocoa were the duty now levied on it repealed. The consumption in 1868 was 0·17 per head. In 1853 it was 0·15, and since that year has varied considerably, the lowest rate being 0·09 in 1857.* The duty on Cocoa is one of those which, according to the recommendation of the Import Duties Committee of 1840, ought long since to have been repealed.

The following are the statistics of the year 1868---9 :†

	Duty.	Quantity Taxed.	Amount Collected.
Cocoa	1d. per lb.	5,939,043 lbs	£24,746
„ Husks & shells ...	2s. per cwt.	10,419 cwts.	1,042
„ Paste or Chocolate	2d. per lb.	191,087 lbs.	1,593

DRIED FRUIT.

It is difficult to assign any valid reason why Curants, Figs, Plums, Prunes, and Raisins should be taxed while

---

* Statistical Abstract 1854 to 1868, pp. 42—43.
† Parliamentary Paper. Sess. 1869. No. 427.

Dates are admitted free of duty. There is nothing to be said in defence of these duties. Upon the principles which have now for some time regulated our fiscal policy they ought long since to have been swept away. The quantity taxed and amount produced in 1868-9* is shown below:—

	Duty. Per Cwt.	Quantity Taxed. Cwts.	Amount Collected. £
Currants	7 0	767,748	268,724
Figs, Plums, & Prunes	7 0	94,231	32,994
Raisins	7 0	369,933	129,483

PATENT MEDICINES.

Although neither meat nor drink, these articles are of very general consumption in many districts and among many classes. It can hardly be affirmed that the duty limits the demand for them. It is invariably added to the price by the maker and wholesale vendor, but in some places competition leads the retailer to forego the demand of the duty from the purchaser, the result being that the former pays the duty in the hope of recouping himself by an increased sale. It is a curious fact that so many people are ready to pay from six to twelve times the value of these articles, merely because they have some special designation. The main items in the cost of their production are the charges paid by their enterprising proprietors in order to advertise their hidden virtues, and make known the marvellous cures which they are said to have per-

---

* Parliamentary Paper, Sess. 1869. No. 129.

formed. The most valid objection to the collection of any portion of the revenue in this way seems to be the fact that, in the minds of ignorant people, the government stamp is considered a voucher for the merits of the medicine to which it is attached. The number of stamps for Medicines issued in 1868-9 was 8,663,685, and the amount collected £66,860.*

PLAYING CARDS.

This tax was probably imposed upon moral considerations. It produced during the last financial year £338 from Customs, and £10,324 from stamps on the home made article.† The insignificant amount collected renders this duty unworthy a place in our system of taxation. It was formerly 1s. 3d. per pack, and was then largely evaded, to remedy which it was reduced to 3d., its present rate. A duty of 21s. per pair was formerly imposed upon dice sold, which was evaded by selling the ivory squares unmarked, leaving the purchaser to perform the operation of marking himself. In consequence of this practice the duty, which had become obsolete, was repealed. Neither morality nor the revenue would suffer if the duty on playing cards were to follow.

GOLD AND SILVER PLATE.

The Customs duty on these articles is rendered necessary by the Stamp duty collected upon home manufactures by the Inland Revenue. The genuine

---

* Parliamentary Paper, Sess. 1869. No. 427.
† Parliamentary Paper, Sess. 1869. No. 427.

nature of the articles is guaranteed by the stamp, and it cannot be said that the duty is productive of any considerable hardship. If the Government undertakes to test and examine quality, it is clearly entitled to a charge sufficient to defray the cost of the establishments necessary for the purpose.

The following is the amount collected in 1868-9.—*

	Duty Per oz. Troy.	Quantity Taxed. Oz. Troy.	Amount Collected. £
Plate of Gold	17s.	120	102
Plate of Silver	1s. 6d.	48015	3,581
Stamps	Same as Customs.	Not stated	65,678

* Parliamentary Paper, Sess. 1869. No. 427.

CHAPTER X.

MALT AND ITS PRODUCTS, WITH THEIR SUBSTITUTES.

The Malt Tax was first imposed in England in 1697, in Scotland in 1713, and in Ireland in 1785. The following statement of the various changes in this duty was handed in to the Select Committee of the House of Commons appointed, in 1867 to enquire into the operation of the Malt Tax, by Mr. Stephenson, the Chairman of the Board of Inland Revenue:—*

	England Per Bushel. s. d.	Scotland Per Bushel. s. d.	Ireland Per Bushel. s. d.
1697	6		
1713	6	6	
1726	6	3	
1760	9¼	3	
1780	1 4¼	8	
1785	1 4¼	8	7
1795	1 4¼	8	1 3
1802	2 5	1 8¾	1 9½
1804	4 5¾	3 9½	2 3½
1813	4 5¾	3 9½	3 3¾
1815	4 5¾	3 9½	4 5
1816	2 5	1 8¾	2 4½
1819	3 7¼	3 7¼	3 6¾
1822	2 7	2 7	2 7
1840	2 8½	2 8½	2 8½
1854	4 0	4 0	4 0
1856	2 8½	2 8½	2 8½

---

* Report of Select Committee on the Malt Tax, Sess. 1868. No. 420, p. iii.

No change has been made since 1856.

In the course of his evidence before the Committee, Mr. Stephenson stated as a remarkable fact, that the consumption of malt had remained almost stationary for 100 years prior to 1830, although the population had largely increased; that during this period it was 25,000,000 bushels a year; and that on the repeal of the beer duty in 1830 the consumption of malt rapidly increased, until in 1866 it reached 45,000,000 bushels for England only. In that year the amount of malt on which duty was paid in the United Kingdom was upwards of 52,000,000 bushels. These statements led the committee to express an opinion that a reduction in the rate of duty would lead to a large increase in the consumption of malt.

In reference to the diminution in the consumption of malt which took place during the last century, Mr. Porter observes* that it would not be correct to attribute that fact entirely to the effect of taxation, the introduction of tea and coffee into extensive use having necessarily interfered with the consumption of beer. The same effect has been produced by the increased consumption of spirits, which it has been alleged was caused to some extent at least, in the early part of the present century, by the exorbitant duties then levied on malt and beer.† There can be no doubt that tea and coffee have proved powerful competitors for public

---

* Progress of the Nation, 1847, p. 563.

† McCulloch Culloch on Taxation, 1845, p. 237.

favour. Their rivalry with ale and beer has, however, been more equal than that of chicory with coffee, excessive duties having been imposed upon both tea and coffee from their first introduction until a recent period, as well as upon sugar, which is generally an important ingredient in the conversion of tea and coffee into beverages.

Mr. Porter describes the tax on malt as one that "has always been unfavourably viewed by the agricultural interest, under the common but unaccountable impression that the amount is paid by the producers, and not, as it in fact is, by the consumers. Under this impression, the endeavour to cause its repeal has at times been strenuously made, and it is probable that it would not always have been made in vain, could any sufficient substitute for the revenue have been found that would not have been even more distasteful to landlords."* The idea that this tax is paid by he producer is somewhat akin to the notion, formerly prevalent in agricultural districts, that taxes upon imports were paid by "the foreigner." Nothing can be more certain than that all such imposts, whether of Customs or Excise, fall upon the consumer, by whom they are ultimately paid. This fact, however, does not disprove the assertion that the Malt Tax is prejudicial to the interests of the farmers. All indirect taxes are more or less injurious to the producers of the articles taxed, whatever may be the benefits they appear to

---

* Progress of the Nation, 1847, p. 565.

confer upon the few capitalists, in whose favour they create a monopoly of trade or manufacture.

The Select Committee of the House of Commons, appointed in 1867, summed up the evidence laid before them in the following words :—*

"Your Committee consider that the result of the evidence taken by them is, that the malt tax prevents the farmer from cultivating his land to the greatest advantage; that it obstructs him in the use of a valuable article of food for cattle; that, by making it necessary to employ a large additional amount of capital in the important trade of malting and brewing, it has created and tends to foster two large monopolies; and that, by materially increasing the price of beer, it encourages adulteration, and prevents to a great extent the habit of brewing amongst the labouring people." This clause of the report was carried by the vote of the Chairman,† the members voting *for* it being Mr. S. Cave, Lord Eustace Cecil, Sir E. Manningham Buller, Mr. Read, Mr. Henry Surtees, and Mr. More. *Against*: Mr. Goschen, Mr. Shaw Lefevre, Mr. Arthur Peel, Mr. Ayrton, Mr. Dent and Mr. Hardcastle. The Chairman, Colonel Barttelot, then voted for the clause.

The views of the minority were stated as follows, in a draft report submitted by Mr. Dent,‡ "the evidence of the officers of Excise, of the malsters, and of the brewers, shows that the tax is one of yearly increasing

---

* Report of Select Committee of the House of Commons on Malt Tax, Sess. 1868. No. 420. p. v.
† Ibid p. xii.
‡ Ibid p. xi.

amount, easily and cheaply collected, and not pressing with harshness upon the operations of trade, nor injuriously affecting the retail price of beer to the consumer." It further stated that the evidence of the corn-dealers, the large brewers, and the buyers of barley tended to throw doubt on the objections raised to the tax by the agriculturists, and after some other remarks expressed unwillingness "to incur the responsibility of disturbing so important a branch of the revenue as the Malt Tax."

An analysis of the division list shows that four of the members who voted for Mr. Dent's draft report have since become members of the present Government, and that the fifth is a brewer. It is mainly based upon the evidence of the officers of Excise, the malsters, the brewers, corn-dealers, and buyers of barley, who were examined before the committee. Its solitary recommendation was to the effect that some relaxation of the law, in favour of the farmer sprouting malt for his cattle, should be considered by the excise; the interest of the Consumer was altogether ignored. As respects the cheapness with which this duty is said to be collected a few remarks will be found on a subsequent page. That a tax is collected "*easily*" is not always an advantage to the taxpayer though it may cause officials to regard it with peculiar favour. As to the evidence upon which the minority rely there is one obvious reply; revenue officers are apt to regard existing taxes as objects deserving their defence and protection; very few dealers in taxed commodities desire the removal of duties on the articles they sell, because the trade would be thereby opened to men of smaller capital than themselves; the evidence of farmers is more trustworthy upon the agricultural part of the question than that of corndealers, brewers, and buyers of barley. No free-trader, or disciple of Richard Cobden, can admit that Mr. Dent's proposed report was deserving of the support it received.

It is manifestly inconsistent with the opinions of Lord John Russell, Mr. C. P. Villiers and Mr. Cobden, as laid before the Committee in the evidence of Mr. Fielden.*

Speaking in 1846, Lord John Russell said: "If I were Prime Minister when protection to agriculture was abolished, the first tax I would repeal would be the Malt Tax." Mr. Villiers declared in 1839, that "all those who were injured by the operation of the Corn Laws would be willing, nay, would be anxious to get rid of the Malt Tax." Mr. Cobden said, as late as 1864, "it has often occurred to me to compare the case of the British agriculturist, who, after raising a bushel of barley, is compelled to pay a tax of 60 per cent. before he is permitted to convert it into a beverage for his own consumption, with what I have seen in foreign countries, and I can really call to mind nothing so hard and so unreasonable. I am quite sure that the cultivators of vineyards and the growers of olives in France and Italy, would never tolerate such treatment of their wine and oil."

---

* Report of Select Committee on the Malt Tax. Session 1868, No. 420, p. 152.

The most astounding assertion in Mr. Dent's draft report was that which stated that the tax is cheaply collected. It is true that the Chairman of the Board of Inland Revenue, in his evidence, estimated the cost of collection at 3 per cent., or about £180,000; but it must be remembered that the actual cost of collection to the consumer is the amount he is made to pay in excess of the natural price of his beer untaxed, *plus* the tax itself. In this instance the consumer pays the profits of the malster, the brewer, and the retailer; the tax being levied at the first stage of manufacture, and its pressure being thereby greatly aggravated. The evidence of Mr. Joshua Fielden (now M.P. for the East West Riding) fixes the extra cost of collection at 45 per cent.,* the tax charged by the retailer to the consumer being 31s. 6d. per quarter of malt consumed, while the amount received by the Exchequer is only 21s. 8d. Mr. Dudley Baxter quotes Mr. Fielden's evidence,† and calculates that, after making allowance for the fervour of Mr. Fielden's opposition to the tax, the increase may be safely taken at 31 per cent. If Mr. Baxter's estimate is taken in preference to that of Mr. Fielden, it will even then be seen that the actual cost of collection is £2,000,000 in excess of the amount stated by Mr. Stephenson. A revenue collected at such a cost ought, in all conscience, to be collected with ease. In these calculations, moreover,

---

* Malt Tax Report, 1868, p. 145.

† The Taxation of the United Kingdom, p. 138.

no account is taken of the extra profits charged by licensed victuallers for beer sold by the pint or glass. A detailed statement of the cost of Customs and Excise was prepared and issued by the Financial Reform Association of Liverpool, in 1852, which entered into minute calculations based upon information collected from brewers, dealers, and other competent authorities. The following table shows the conclusion arrived at in the case of beer. The figures are based upon the returns of 1850 :—

	£
Cost to public free of duty including profits	32,558,530
Net amount of duty on Malt and Hops	4,232,931
Direct and Indirect cost of collecting the revenue...	9,888,714
	46,680,175

In addition the writer estimated £125,745 as the extra charges on malt and hops used in private families. It is evident that the last calculation includes full profits on consumption over the counter in small quantities. It appears that the three estimates vary from 31 to above 200 per cent.; whichever may be adopted as the standard it cannot be said with accuracy that this tax is collected at a small expense.

The imposition of duties upon malt and beer has been defended on the ground that, by restricting consumption, they check intemperance. There are, however, two sides to this aspect of the question. Opponents of the Malt Tax urge that it is a powerful incentive to the intemperate use of malt liquors in consequence of the adulterations to which it gives rise.

They allege that beer sold at public houses is rarely to be had in a pure state; that it excites instead of quenching thirst; that this adulteration is mainly caused by the high duty on malt; and that a large proportion of the evils of intemperance are attributable thereto. It is an ascertained fact that excessive duties upon articles of consumption have a direct tendency to encourage adulteration, which in the case of beer takes the form of increasing the apparent strength of the beverage. It is a question deserving of consideration by all who desire to promote habits of temperance, whether the increased consumption of pure malt liquor would not be far preferable to the consumption of Nux Vomica, Cocculus Indicus, Grains of Paradise, and some thirty other ingredients, which are described by writers on temperance as being largely employed in the adulteration of beer.

It does not appear, from the demand now made for the more stringent regulation of public houses, that the existing laws, although aided by high taxes on beer and spirits, have been effective for their purpose. It may be well, therefore, to reconsider the whole question. It seems to be a curious and anomalous step to endeavour to promote sobriety by making the Government a partner, to so large an extent, in the profits derived from the sale of intoxicating drinks; it may yet be discovered that such a policy is a mistake, and that the raising of a considerable portion of the National Revenue from such sources is by no means an effective way of checking intemperance.

The amount of duty levied on malt during the year 1868-9 was as follows :—*

	Duty. Per bushel.	Quantities. Bushels.	Amount. £
Excise.	s. d.		
Made from barley...	2 7 } and 5 per cent	49,542,938 }	6,724,255
„ bere or bigg...	2 0 } additional.	47,572 }	
Customs.			
Isle of Man	... 25 0 per quarter	32 qrs. 4 bush.	41
Foreign ...	... 25 0 per quarter	—	—
			£6,724,296

The Importation of Foreign Malt was prohibited prior to the year 1850; it is now admitted at a duty of 25s. per quarter, the excess over the Tax levied on British Malt being an equivalent for the licenses and expenses caused by the supervision of the excise. The quantity of malt imported is very insignificant, and, according to the evidence adduced before the committee, there is considerable variety of opinion as to the probable effect of the repeal of the duty upon the importation of malt from abroad.

The following table shows the average consumption of malt per head at various periods during the present century.*

1801	1·20	1852	1·50
1811	1·60	1855	1·24
1821	1·38	1859	1·67
1831	1·63	1862	1·50
1838	1·56	1864	1·75
1840	1·60	1866	1·82
1841	1·35	1868	1·73

---

* Parliamentary Paper, "Taxes and Imposts," Sess. 1869. No. 427.
* Porters' Progress of the Nation, 1847, p. 561. Statistical Abstract 11th No. 1867, p. 42. Ibid, 16th No., 1868, pp. 42, 43.

The average consumption of each individual in each decennary year from 1740 to 1790 was as follows :—*

1740	3·78	1770	3·38
1750	4·85	1780	3·94
1760	4·29	1790	2·57

The repeal of the duty on malt, without any equivalent, appears to be abandoned by the warmest opponents of the tax. It has powerful rivals for the favour of the Chancellor of the Exchequer in tea, coffee, and sugar, and there seems little prospect of the repeal of the malt tax until the Free Breakfast Table has become an accomplished fact. The Report of the Select Comittee recommends its commutation into a tax upon the manufacture of beer. From this the minority dissent on the ground that such a change would involve considerably more trouble in the collection, and great risk to the revenue, without any sufficient advantage. If a substitute for this impost is required it may fairly be looked for in the direction of that tax upon real property in lieu of which one half the Excise was, in the reign of Charles the Second, settled upon the King and his heirs for ever. If the complaints of the agriculturists are well founded, it must be evident that the removal of the duty on malt would have the inevitable result of increasing the rental of the Landowners. They have not suffered any diminution of income in consequence of Free Trade, nor is Agriculture less prosperous than it was under Protection, when its distressed condition was the

---

* Porter's Progress of the Nation 1847, p. 564.

topic of constant Parliamentary discussion. On the contrary, both Landlords and Tenants have vastly benefited by every development of the Free Trade policy. If the representatives of the County Constituencies are in earnest in desiring the repeal of this tax, nothing is more easy of accomplishment. They have merely to consent to a direct tax upon property, which would be amply repaid them in enhanced rentals, if their statements as to the prejudicial effects of the tax upon agriculture have any foundation in fact.

The following duties are charged upon "products of malt, with their substitutes:"*

	Duty £	Quantity Taxed. Brls. Galls.	Amount Collected. £
Customs.			
Beer, Mum	1 per barrel	3 30	4
Spruce	1 per barrel	1,666 31	1,667
Beer and ale of other sorts	1 per barrel	2,537 21	2,533
		Value. £	
Essence of Spruce	10 per cent. ad. val.	7	1
		Gallons.	
Vinegar	3d. per gallon	52,242	653
Pickles preserved in ditto	1d. per gallon	1,816	8
Excise.			
Beer relanded, return of drawback on exportation		Barrels. 193	68
			£4,934

* Parliamentary Paper, "Taxes and Imposts," Session 1869, No. 427.

CHAPTER II.

LICENSES ON TRADES AND PROFESSIONS.

Licenses have been required in this country mainly in the case of manufacturers of, and dealers in, taxed commodities, for the alleged purpose of protecting the revenue. The levy of Excise duties necessitates supervision of the processes of manufacture; hence, in order that all makers of exciseable articles might be known readily, the burden of a license duty was added to that of the tax upon the manufacture itself. In some cases licenses are employed for purposes of police regulation. They have never been imposed in this country, as in France, upon traders generally, owing to the difficulty of assessing them in an equitable manner. If the license is uniform, it must press much more heavily upon the small than upon the large trader. Assessment, according to the extent of business transacted, or the size of the premises occupied, is difficult, and, even were that plan adopted, such a tax would necessarily partake of the nature of a tax on profits.

The licenses now levied upon manufacturers are as follows :*—

Manufacturers.	Duty. £ s. d.	No. of Licenses.	Amount. £ s.
Brewers	various	35,664	355,672 5
Maltsters	various	5,494	15,425 8
Manufacturers of Tobacco and Snuff	various	597	7,512 15
Distillers of Spirits	10 10 0	142	1,491 0
Rectifiers of ditto	10 10 0	163	1,711 10
Makers of Methylated Spirits	10 10 0	9	94 10
Papermakers	4 4 0	408	1,713 12
Soapmakers	4 4 0	308	1,293 12
Roasters of Malt	20 0 0	21	420 0
Vinegar Makers	5 5 0	63	330 15
Makers of Playing Cards	1 0 0	14	14 0
Makers of Stills in Scotland and Ireland	10 6	18	9 9

The license duties upon brewers are levied according to the number of barrels brewed, the following being the present scale of duties:—

Brewers of black or spruce beer, various rates from 10s. 6d. to £78 15s. 0d. according to the quantities brewed.
Brewers of beer, other than black or spruce,
   beginners 0 12 6
Quantity brewed not exceeding 20 barrels ... 0 12 6
Exceeding 20 and not exceeding 50 barrels ... 1 7 6
  „ 50 100 „ ... 2 0 0
  „ 100 1,000 for every 50 or fractional part of 50 barrels over 100 barrels 0 15 0
Exceeding 1,000 and not exceeding 50,000 in addition to the above, for every 50, or fractional part of 50 barrels over 1,000 ... 0 14 0
Exceeding 50,000 barrels, in addition to the foregoing, for every 50 or fractional part of 50 barrels 0 12 6
Brewers using sugar 1 0 0
Retail brewers under Act 5, Geo. IV., c 54. ... 5 10 3

* Parliamentary Paper, "Taxes and Imposts." Session 1869, No. 427.

The present scale was adopted in the year 1862, when the duty on hops was repealed, an addition being then made to the brewer's license, calculated at the rate of 3d. per barrel of 36 gallons, which sum was considered the minimum duty paid by the brewer upon hops. At the same time the scale of licenses upon small brewers was revised, it being found to press more heavily upon them than upon those who had larger establishments.

The substitution of the additional license duty for the tax on hops, removed an element of uncertainty from the annual budgets of the Chancellor of the Exchequer. It will be seen from the table on the next page, which was handed in to the Malt Tax Committee by Mr. Curling of the Inland Revenue, that during the ten years preceding the repeal of the duty it fluctuated from £728,183 to £69,767, and that during the same period the duty on brewers' licenses was stationary. Since the year 1862, the revenue from that source has steadily increased.*

The diminished receipt since the repeal of the hop duty is owing partly to the fact that private brewers pay no license duty, and have thus been relieved entirely from taxation on account of hops; and partly to the calculation of 3d. per barrel being made upon the quantity of hops used in ordinary brewing; so that brewers of bitter beer have been relieved entirely from any duty upon the extra hops they use.

---

* Malt Tax Report, 1867, p. 141.

Year	Duty on Brewers' Licenses. £	Hop Duty. £	Total Brewers' Licenses & Hop Duty. £	Total Brewers' Licenses. £
1852	80,611	447,143	527,754	
1853	82,342	277,807	360,149	
1854	79,887	86,422	166,309	
1855	76,646	728,183	804,829	
1856	78,167	488,850	567,017	
1857	79,493	417,526	497,019	
1858	78,464	464,842	543,306	
1859	80,662	599,346	680,008	
1860	80,928	69,767	150,695	
1861	77,814	149,709	227,523	
1862	302,403			302,403
1863	353,541			353,541
1864	378,092			378,092
1865	384,966			384,966
1866	443,080			443,080
Total	2,657,096	3,729,595	4,524,609	1,862,082
Average of ten years			452,461	
Average of five years				372,416

It was proposed by some witnesses before the Malt Tax Committee to increase the license duty upon brewers, as a substitute for the malt tax. This suggestion was met by the revenue officers with the assertion, that it would be impossible to guarantee the collection of the duty, if the license was increased to such an extent, without completely altering all their arrangements, and subjecting the brewers to a more thorough supervision. It was also considered that the difficulty of imposing a license upon private brewers, an illustration of which was afforded by the failure of that proposal when the hop duty was repealed, would render it impossible to carry through Parliament such a commutation of the duty on malt.

The following is the scale of license duty paid by malsters:*—

		£	s.	d.
Beginners, with a surcharge according to the quantity made...			7	10½
Quantity made not exceeding 50 quarters			7	10½
,, ,, 100 ,,			15	9
,, ,, 150 ,,		1	3	7½
,, ,, 200 ,,		1	11	6
,, ,, 250 ,,		1	19	4½
,, ,, 300 ,,		2	7	3
,, ,, 350 ,,		2	15	1½
,, ,, 400 ,,		3	3	0
,, ,, 450 ,,		3	10	10½
,, ,, 500 ,,		3	18	9
,, ,, 550 ,,		4	6	7½
Quantity made exceeding 550 ,,		4	14	6
Bye Maltsters, not exceeding 5 ,,			2	7½

The following are the licenses paid by manufacturers of tobacco and snuff:†—

	£	s.	d.
Beginners with a surcharge according to quantity manufactured	5	5	0
Quantity ,, not exceeding 20,000 lbs.	5	5	0
,, ,, ,, 40,000 ,,	10	10	0
,, ,, ,, 60,000 ,,	15	15	0
,, ,, ,, 80,000 ,,	21	0	0
,, ,, ,, 100,000 ,,	26	5	0
,, ,, exceeding 100,000 ,,	31	10	0

---

* Parliamentary Paper, "Taxes and Imposts." Session 1869, No. 427.
† Ibid.

The brewer's license is intended to act as a tax on beer, and there is no doubt it is paid by the consumer, like other duties on commodities. It is difficult, however, to understand why tobacco manufacturers and malsters, both of whose products are heavily taxed, should pay a graduated scale of license duties, while distillers and rectifiers of spirits pay one uniform license, whatever the extent of their business. If it be urged in reply to this objection, that the larger the business the greater the supervision required for the protection of the revenue, the tobacco manufacturer and malster may fairly answer that that is no concern of theirs. They are already sufficiently burdened in their business by the imposition of a heavy duty upon their manufacture, which renders it necessary for them to provide a capital out of all proportion to the extent of their business. Makers of soap and paper may also enquire why they should be specially selected to pay license duties, from which other manufacturers are exempt.

BEER, SPIRIT, AND WINE DEALERS AND RETAILERS.

Licenses for the sale of intoxicating drinks being levied not for the collection of a revenue, but mainly as a matter of police regulation, it is not intended to enter upon the discussion of them in this volume. Even were there space sufficient for the purpose, such a controversy would be somewhat out of place in a work dealing solely with the collection of the revenue. It appears tolerably certain that a great change in the system of licensing public houses is imminent; the pressing nature of the problem is admitted by men of all parties, and whatever may be the proposals made, considerations of the amount of revenue to be derived will have but little weight in the discussion. The following table shows the existing scale of licenses, the number issued, and the total gross sum received from this source.*

Description of License.	Rate. £ s. d.	Number.	Total Gross Sum Produced. £ s. d.
Beer Dealers :—			
Sellers of strong beer in quantities not less than 4½ gallons, or two dozen reputed quart bottles ..	3 6 1¾	5,952	19,684 19 11¾
Sellers of strong beer to retail; not to be consumed on the premises	1 2 ½	3,820	4,209 19 2
Beer Retailers :—			
Publicans whose premises are rated under £20 per annum in England and Ireland	1 2 ½	41,923	46,202 12 9½
Publicans rated at £20 or upwards..	3 6 1¾	43,491	143,837 8 5¼
Retailers of beer not to be drunk on the premises in England and Wales	1 2 ½	3,460	3,813 4 2
Retailers of beer to be drunk on the premises..	3 6 1¾	49,130	162,487 4 9¼
Retailers of cyder or perry only	1 2 ½	368	405 11 4
Retailers of beer rated under £10 in Scotland	2 10 0	299	747 10 0
Retailers of beer rated at £10 or upwards	4 4 0	274	1,150 16 0
Retailers of table beer only	0 5 0	2,720	680 0 0
Spirit Dealers :—			
Dealers in spirits, to sell not less than two gals.	10 10 0	5,894	61,887 0 0
Dealers in spirits, to retail foreign liqueurs	2 2 0	6	12 12 0
Dealers in spirits, to retail spirits, not less than one quart bottle	3 3 0	2,894	9,116 2 0

* Parliamentary Paper " Taxes and Imposts." Session 1869, No. 427.

Description of License.	Rate. £ s. d.	Number.	Total Gross Sum Produced. £ s. d.
Spirit Retailers:—			
England and Ireland:			
Retailers of spirits whose premises are rated—			
under £10	2 4 1		
At £10 and under £20	4 8 2½		
£20 „ £25	6 12 3½		
£25 „ £30	7 14 4	83,984	539,208 9 7¼
£30 „ £40	8 16 4¾		
£40 „ £50	9 18 5¼		
£50 or upwards ..	11 0 6		
Scotland only:			
Retailers of spirits whose premises are rated—			
under £10	4 4 0		
At £10 and under £20	5 5 0		
£20 „ £25	9 9 0		
£25 „ £30	10 10 0	12,022	84,571 4 0
£30 „ £40	11 11 0		
£40 „ £50	12 12 0		
£50 or upwards ..	13 13 0		
Ireland only:			
Retailers of spirits being licensed to sell tea, coffee, &c., whose premises are rated—under £25	9 18 5¼		
At £25 and under £30	11 0 6		
£30 „ £40	12 2 6¼	434	4,699 14 8¼
£40 „ £50	13 4 7		
£50 or upwards ..	14 6 7¾		
Retailers of Methylated Spirits	0 10 0	1,180	590 0 0
Wine Dealers:—			
Dealers in foreign wine, not licensed to retail beer or spirits	10 10 0	3,639	38,209 10 0
Dealers in foreign wine, licensed to retal beer but not spirits	4 8 2¼	69	301 4 10¼
Dealers in foreign wine, licensed to retail beer and spirits	2 4 1	43,779	96,496 4 3
Scotland only:			
Grocers selling wine not to be consumed on the premises, having the justices' certificate to retail beer but not spirits	4 8 2¼	24	105 16 6

Description of License.	Rate £ s. d.	Number.	Total Gross Sum Produced. £ s. d.
Grocers selling wine not to be consumed on the premises, having the justices' certificate to retail spirits only	—	—	—
Grocers selling wine not to be consumed on the premises, having the justices' certificate to retail beer and spirits	2 4 1	2,050	4,518 10 10
England and Ireland: Refreshment-housekeepers selling wine to be consumed on the premises—			
If rated under £50 ..	3 3 0	2,153	6,781 19 0
If rated at £50 or upwards	5 5 0	821	4,310 5 0
Retailers of wine not to be consumed on the premises—			
If rated under £50	2 2 0	2,098	4,405 16 0
If rated at £50 or upwards	3 3 0	608	1,915 4 0
Passage vessels for sale of liquors and tobacco ..	1 1 0	374	392 14 0

The remaining licenses levied upon trades and professions are the following :—*

	Duty. £ s. d.	No.	£ s.
Refreshment Houses rated under £30	10 6	2,812	1,476 6
At £30 and upwards	1 1 0	3,595	3,774 15
Dealers in Tobacco	5 3	284,124	74,582 11
Dealers in Sweets, to sell not less 2 gals.	5 5 0	123	645 15
Retailers of Sweets...	1 2 0½	10,441	11,506 17
Dealers in Roasted Malt	10 0 0	12	120 0
Hawkers and Pedlars	various from £2 in Gt. Britain £2 2s. Ireland	20,740	52,095 0
Appraisers & House Agents	2 0 0	3,922	7,844 0

* Parliamentary Paper "Taxes and Imposts." Sess. 1869. No. 427.

	Duty. £ s. d.	No.	£ s.
Auctioneers	10 0 0	5,276	52,760 0
Pawnbrokers:—			
In London	15 0 0 }	3,918	33,067 10
Elsewhere	7 10 0 }		
Dealers in Plate:—			
To sell 2 oz. gold or 30 oz. silver & upwards	5 15 0 }	9,521	29,716 0
To sell 2 dwts. gold or more than 5 dwts. silver, and under 2 oz. gold and 30 oz. silver	2 6 0 }		
Sellers of Playing Cards	2 6	8,748	1,093 10
Medicine Vendors:			
In London and Edinburgh	2 0 0 }	12,271	6,842 10
Other cities, boros', or towns corporate in Gt. Britain	0 10 0 }		
Elsewhere in Gt. Britain	5 0 }		
Chemists and others using stills	10 0	839	419 10
Stamps:—			
Attornies, &c.			
London, Edinboro', & Dublin	9 0 0 yearly }	13,475	90,301 10
Elsewhere	6 0 0 " }		
	Half only for the first three years of practice.		
Bankers	30 0 0 yearly	1,172	35,160 0
Conveyancers	same as Attornies.	72	517 10
Drivers of Metropolitan public carriages	5 0	12,144	3,186 0
Taxes:—			
Horse dealers	Carrying on business within the bounds of mortality £27 10s. Elsewhere 13 15s.	57 } 1,199 }	17,746 0

It is difficult to understand the *raison d'etre* of some of the above licenses. The only class who have hitherto made any complaint are the attorneys, but as yet they have been unsuccessful in obtaining any relief. The multiplication of small and comparatively unproductive taxes is no doubt attended with increased cost of collection. It would seem, moreover, just, unless there are any special reasons for continuing any particular licenses, that the system should either be extended to all trades and professions, or abrogated. At some future time, when more serious and injurious burdens have been removed, it is probable that the number of license duties will be materially reduced.

CHAPTER XII.

PROBATE, LEGACY, AND SUCCESSION DUTIES.

Stamp duties upon grants of probate and administration were first imposed in England in 1694, at the rate of 5s. upon every grant of probate or administration of property above £20 in value. The duty was increased four years afterwards to 10s., at which rate it continued for above 85 years, until August 1779, when an ascending scale was imposed, reaching as far as property of the value of £300; the scale was increased in 1783, and extended as far as property of the value of £1,000. The same process was repeated in 1789, in 1795, and in 1801, when the rates of duty were largely increased, and the ascending scale of duty extended as far as property of the value of £100,000. In 1804 the scale of duties was again revised, and extended so as to reach property of the value of £500,000, and in 1815 the present scale of duties was adopted, stopping, however, at £1,000,000. It was extended to property above that amount in 1859. Prior to the year 1815 the duty on probates and letters of administration was the same; the duty on the latter was then increased in the proportion of 3 to 2, thus taxing the property of an intestate one-third more than that of a testator.*

The probate duty was first imposed in Ireland in 1774 at 5s. for each grant of probate or administration exceeding £30 in value. The amount of the tax was subsequently increased by different Acts until 1806, but at a lower rate than in England. In 1842 the English rates were imposed in Ireland, but only temporarily; in 1853 they were made permanent. No tax of this description existed in Scotland until 1804, when the same rate was imposed as in England, but practically the tax was not equally paid in both countries. The various alterations made in the rate of probate duty are a test of the gradually increasing wealth of the community. According to the successive Probate Tax Acts, the probable limit of accumulation of personality appears to have been as follows for each of the specified periods:—

		£
1779 to 1783	...	300
1783 „ 1789	...	1,000
1789 „ 1795	...	5,000
1795 „ 1801	...	10,000
1801 „ 1804	...	100,000
1804 „ 1815	...	500,000
1815 „ 1859	...	1,000,000

In 1859 the possibility of accumulations exceeding £1,000,000 was first recognised. The earlier years are in all probability no adequate test of accumulation, but since 1801 the scale appears to have been

---

* First Inland Revenue Report, 1857, App. p. 22.

extended as the number of large fortunes increased. The number of probate stamps issued of the "upper value" (£1,000,000) from 1815 to 1860 was twelve. From 1815 to 1825 none were required. From 1825 to 1855 there were issued eight; and from 1855 to 1860 four, the last being issued in June 1859, just before the extension of the scale.*

The following is the present scale of duties:—§

Value			With Will annexed.	Without a Will annexed.
£		£	£ s.	£ s.
Above 20	and under	50		0 10
,, 20	,,	100	0 10	
of 50		100		1
100	,,	200	2	3
200	,,	300	5	8
300	,,	450	8	11
450	,,	600	11	15
600	,,	800	15	22
800	,,	1,000	22	30
1,000	,,	1,500	30	45
1,500	,,	2,000	40	60
2,000	,,	3,000	50	75
3,000	,,	4,000	60	90
4,000	,,	5,000	80	120
5,000	,,	6,000	100	150
6,000	,,	7,000	120	180
7,000	,,	8,000	140	210
8,000	,,	9,000	160	240
9,000	,,	10,000	180	270
10,000	,,	12,000	200	300
12,000	,,	14,000	220	330
14,000	,,	16,000	250	375
16,000	,,	18,000	280	420
18,000	,,	20,000	310	465
20,000	,,	25,000	350	525

* Fourth Inland Revenue Report, 1860, p. 17.
§ First Inland Revenue Report, 1857, App. p. 101. Act 22 & 23 Vic., c. 36., s. 1.

Value			With Will annexed. £	Without a Will annexed. £
£		£		
25,000	,,	30,000	400	600
30,000	,,	35,000	450	675
35,000	,,	40,000	525	785
40,000	,,	45,000	600	900
45,000	,,	50,000	675	1,010
50,000	,,	60,000	750	1,125
60,000	,,	70,000	900	1,350
70,000	,,	80,000	1,050	1,575
80,000	,,	90,000	1,200	1,800
90,000	,,	100,000	1,350	2,025
100,000	,,	120,000	1,500	2,250
120,000	,,	140,000	1,800	2,700
140,000	,,	160,000	2,100	3,150
160,000	,,	180,000	2,400	3,600
180,000	,,	200,000	2,700	4,050
200,000	,,	250,000	3,000	4,500
250,000	,,	300,000	3,750	5,625
300,000	,,	350,000	4,500	6,750
350,000	,,	400,000	5,250	7,875
400,000	,,	500,000	6,000	9,000
500,000	,,	600,000	7,500	11,250
600,000	,,	700,000	9,000	13,500
700,000	,,	800,000	15,000	15,750
800,000	,,	900,000	12,000	18,000
900,000	,,	1,000,000	13,500	20,250
1,000,000 and upwards, then for every £100,000, or portion thereof, an additional duty of			1,500	2,250

There are several inequalities in the assessment of this duty, which render it peculiarly deserving the early consideration of the Chancellor of the Exchequer. Sixteen years since, Mr. Gladstone, in the Financial Statement of 1853, admitted that the probate duty required reform, and expressed a hope that in a future and early year it would come under consideration. The public has waited with patience for the practical realisation of this anticipation, but with the exception of the extension of the duty to properties beyond £1,000,000 in value nothing has yet been done.

The most obvious grievance connected with this tax is the fact that it is exacted from personal property only, no probate duty being levied upon real estate, whatever its value. The personalty of the struggling tradesman is taxed; the more valuable and permanent real estate of the wealthy landed proprietor escapes. It is difficult to imagine on what grounds the exemption of the latter can be justified; it certainly is not in accordance with those principles of equity which should regulate the action of Government. The next grievance is the assessment of large estates at a lower rate than small ones. For example, the probate duty upon £1,000 is 3 per cent, upon £10,000 it is 2 per cent, and upon £50,000 it is only 1½ per cent. This mode of framing a graduated scale imposes the heaviest burden upon those who have the least means; it is an injustice towards the inheritors of the smaller legacies. Another grievance is the payment of probate upon the full amount of the property, including all debts owing to, "without deducting or allowing anything on account of the debts due and owing from the deceased."* The excess of duty paid is to be returned if claimed within three years, or within such further time as the Lords of the Treasury may consider reasonable. Mr.

---

* 55 Geo. III. c. 184, sec. 38.

Mc Culloch said with justice in 1845*, that "in the case (and there must be many such) of a small tradesman whose debts and credits nearly balance, and are (say) about £2,000, it is surely a wanton and most oppressive misapplication of a tax on successions to make his family provisionally disburse £60 for the privilege of winding up his affairs." This case moreover assumes that the duty paid is returned, which in many instances it is not, the trouble and expense of obtaining it being frequently equal to, if not greater than, the actual amount of the duty. The author is cognizant of an instance of this kind in which the probate duty was actually paid by a creditor, who was also the executor; the Solicitor acting on his behalf informing him that the expense of recovering the duty would absorb the amount recovered. The Commissioners of Inland Revenue refer to this question, in their report for the year 1865—6,† at some length, but strongly protest against any change in the mode of assessing these duties on the ground that it would open the door to fraud. In corroboration of this opinion they refer to attempts, which they allege have been made by executors, to include fictitious debts in claims for return of probate duty. It is, however, a question deserving of some consideration at their hands whether equity on the part of the State would not stimulate honesty on the part of the taxpayer. Danger to the revenue is the invariable stock objection urged against improvement of every description; previous experience has

---

* Taxation and the Funding System, 1845, p. 294.
† Tenth Inland Revenue Revenue Report, 1866, pp.29—32.

repeatedly demonstrated its futility. Revenue authorities are slow to act upon the motto, *fiat justitia ruat cœlum*; if they err at all it is on the side of excessive caution, especially if change is likely to give extra trouble. In this as in previous instances they will no doubt find themselves quite capable of protecting the revenue, whenever the change they now protest against is demanded by public opinion.

Equally unjustifiable is the increased rate imposed upon letters of administration. The absence of a will, which in itself is generally a source of difficulty and trouble to the survivors of the deceased, is thus seized upon by the law as an occasion of extorting an additional amount of taxation. It may be urged in defence of this imposition that the fact of the increased tax will induce people to make their wills. The punishment, however, does not fall upon those who have neglected this duty, but upon innocent sufferers from the neglect. It does not appear that there is any reason for an increased charge on account of extra trouble caused in the collection of the duty; the difference is not founded either on reason or justice, and it ought in common with the exemption of real property to be at once abolished. If probate duties are levied at all, every description of property should be made to contribute in a fair and equitable manner.

The legacy duty was first imposed in Great Britain in 1780, when stamps were required on receipts for legacies; the amount was increased in 1783, and again in 1789. The charge of this duty on the receipt was discovered to be a mistake, so far as making it a source of revenue was concerned, in consequence of a case where it was judicially held that, no receipt having been given, no duty was payable. It was therefore necessary to amend the law in order to make the tax a productive source of revenue; and an act was passed in 1796 by which the duty was imposed upon the legacy instead of the receipt. In 1804 the rates of duty were increased; in 1805 the tax was extended to children and their issue, and increased in the case of strangers in blood; duties were also imposed upon legacies charged upon real estate, or paid from monies arising from real estate directed by the will to be sold. In 1815 the rates of duty were further increased; no change has been made since that year. In Ireland it was first imposed in 1785; it was continued and increased by several subsequent acts, but always at a lower rate than in Great Britain, until 1842, when the rates were made uniform throughout the United Kingdom.*

The collection of the legacy duty from personal property only was the subject of frequent complaints on the part of the trading and manufacturing interests. This injustice was brought before the notice of Parliament with great perseverance by the late Mr. Williams; but for a long time his efforts were unattended by any apparent success. At length, however, in 1853 Mr. Gladstone introduced and carried through Parliament a succession duty on real estate. It was the intention

---

* First Inland Revenue Report, 1857. App. p. xxiii.

of Mr. Pitt, when he introduced the legacy duty act of 1796, to tax both real and personal estate. Unfortunately the two duties were embodied in separate bills, the result being that Parliament passed the legacy duty on personal property only, while the bill for charging duties on real estate being strongly opposed, was ultimately withdrawn, in consequence of one of its last stages being carried only by the casting vote of the speaker. The injustice thus perpetrated was perpetuated for fifty seven years, and then only partially redressed.

The following are the existing rates of duty:—*

	Where the Legacy shall be £20 or more. Per cent.
To children and descendants	1
Father or mother, or any lineal ancestor	1
Brother or sister, or descendants	3
Brother or sister of a father or mother, or their descendants	5
Brother or sister of a grandfather or grandmother, or their descendants	6
Any other collateral relatives, or strangers in blood	10

The rates of duty upon legacies and successions, although nominally the same, are actually different; upon personal property the tax is assessed on the full value, while upon real estate it is assessed on the life interest only of the legatee. The difference was forcibly illustrated by Mr. Bright, in 1859,† in the

---

* First Inland Revenue Report, 1857. App. p. ciii.
† Speeches, edited by James E. Thorold Rogers, 1868. Vol, 2, pp. 401—8.

House of Commons. After stating that he had had a small property left him by a stranger in admiration of his public services, which he sold for £1,400 or £1,500, he added " when I came to pay my legacy duty—that is, the succession tax—I was greatly astonished at the small sum I had to pay. My age was taken; an estimate of the annual value of the property was made; and I was told that I had to pay something like £40 or £50. If the property had been in the funds, or invested in any other of the modes to which I have referred (viz. railways, ships, machinery, or trade), I should have had to pay £140 at least." Mr. Bright adduced another instance in which a property, value £32,000, was left to a member of the House, on which the duty, had it been in personalty, would have been £3,200; but being real estate the amount paid was only £700. He then appealed to the House in the following forcible words:—" Is it consistent with fairness—with our personal honour—for after all that is a quality which enters into these questions—with our duty to the public, that we, sitting here as a representative body, should take one class of property, the most solid and durable, attracting to it the largest social and political advantages, having in it the greatest certainty of accumulation and improvement from the general improvement in the condition of the people, and charge it to the extent of £700, while at the same time we impose £3,200 upon another class of property not more valuable and far more fleeting in its character?" From the fact that no change has yet been made in the law, it appears that a majority of the members of the House do not consider their "personal honour" involved in the matter.

The assessment of the duty on real property according to life interest and not, as in the case of personalty, upon the full value, was defended by Mr. Gladstone,[*] in proposing the succession duty, on the ground that real property bears special burdens in the shape of local taxation. At the same time he proposed to alter and amend the whole foundation of the law, by declaring that whatever exemption or partial advantage was given to real property should be given, in conjunction with it, to other property which was subjected to similar burdens. By this alteration leasehold and copyhold properties were relieved from probate duty and assessed to the succession, instead of the legacy, duty.

Mr. Gladstone estimated that the succession duty would add £500,000 to the revenue for the year 1853—4; a further increase of £700,000 for the year 1854—5; £400,000 for the year 1855-6; and £400,000 more for the year 1856—7 making a total addition to the permanent taxation of the country of not less than £2,000,000 per annum.[†] The following table shows to what extent his anticipations were realised.[‡]

---

[*] Financial Statements, 1863, pp. 64—66.   [†] Ibid, p. 67.

[‡] Second Inland Revenue Report, 1858. App. p. v.

Year ending Jan. 5.	Amount paid for Legacy and Succession Duties. £	Amount estimated by Mr. Gladstone in 1853. £
1854	1,383,922	...
Year ending March 31.		
1855	1,530,843	1,883,922
1856	1,712,785	2,583,922
1857	1,880,988	2,983,922
1858	1,864,725	3,383,932

It appears, therefore, that the amount received in 1856-7 was £1,519,207 less than the estimate. In the following year the receipt showed an actual decrease of £16,263. The Commissioners confessed their inability to account for this fact; the Controller of Legacy Duties attributed it to the remission of duties legally payable, the high value of money during the latter part of the year, and pending litigation of questions under the Succession Duty Act, which was described as having been "most unscrupulous and incessant."* The last named fact says little for the framing of the Act, or for the willingness of landed proprietors to pay the new duty.

The only remission of duty, legally payable, of any importance in 1858 arose in connection with the eleventh section of the Succession Duty Act, which placed a son in-law or daughter-in-law on the same footing as a son or daughter in blood, reducing the duty on such legacies from ten per cent. to one per cent. The benefit was limited by the clause to property

---

† Second Inland Revenue Report, 1858, pp. 20-23.

inherited under the will of a person dying after the passing of the Act. It soon became apparent that the limitation could not be maintained, and authority was obtained from the Treasury to consider the provisions of the Act applicable to the cases of all legacies thereafter charged with duty, without reference to the date of the testator's death.

The accounts of monies received on legacy and succession duties were not kept distinct until the year 1860, when it appears that the amounts were—

Legacy Duty	£1,528,245
Succession Duty	601,775
Total	£2,130,020*

The Reports of the Inland Revenue Commissioners since 1858 contain little respecting these duties but records of litigation. The amount they produce varies considerably, according as the estates brought under charge are large or small. They have been materially affected since 1866 by the depreciation of shares in public companies which followed the panic of that year. The following are the amounts realised during the last four financial years :—†

Year ending 31st March.	Legacy and Succession Duty. £
1866	2,604,332
1867	2,568,044
1868	2,882,748
1869	2,784,997
Average	£2,710,030

* Fourth Inland Revenue Report, 1860, p. 16.
† Twelfth Inland Revenue Report, Appendix, p. 4; Parliamentary Paper, Session 1869, No. 427.

being still less by the sum of £673,902 than the amount anticipated by Mr. Gladstone.

The most recent Reports of the Inland Revenue Commissioners give the following details of the property assessed at each rate of duty to the legacy and the succession duties. The totals were as follows:*—

Year.	Legacy Duty. £	Succession Duty. £
1865-6	75,890,324	30,815,686
1866-7	74,383,693	31,893,430
1867-8	88,069,712	35,143,007

The return professes to give the "amount of property on which duty was paid," but, inasmuch as the legacy duty is assessed upon the full value, while succession duty is assessed upon the life interest only, the table is useless for estimating the pressure of the tax on personalty as compared with realty.

It was, no doubt, a considerable achievement on the part of Mr. Gladstone to carry through a Parliament composed mainly of landed proprietors, a tax upon the succession of estates, which his great predecessor, Mr. Pitt, was unable to persuade their ancestors to accept. He would have been equally unsuccessful but for the fact that popular support was secured by a large relaxation of the customs tariff, and of duties of excise, which relieved the country from above £2,600,000 of more oppressive taxation. The budget was violently opposed by the minority, by whom it was stigmatised as a war against property and a blow at the Constitu-

---

* Eleventh Inland Revenue Report, 1867, App. p. 11. Twelfth ditto, 1869, App. p. 11.

tion. The magnitude of the injustice which the succession duty of 1853 partially remedied, may be estimated from the fact that during the period commencing with the repeal of the income tax in 1816, and its re-enactment in 1842, the only taxes levied directly upon real property were the Land Tax, producing about £1,000,000, and the stamp duty on deeds and instruments, one-half of which is probably paid by real estate. In other words, out of a revenue of £52,000,000 collected in 1841, real property contributed little more than £1,500,000. It is true that owners of real property paid indirect taxes, in common with other taxpayers, but they had not then learnt the important lesson that it is but a short-sighted policy to impose oppressive burdens upon trade and industry, and thus prevent the development of their own wealth, by checking the productive power of the community.

In estimating the value of the argument in favour of a reduced assessment of land to the succession duty on the ground of local burdens, there are several facts, material to the issue, which the advocates of the existing arrangement are apt to overlook. Many of the local taxes, such as highway, paving, and sewer rates, are in reality payments for improvements which render the property assessed available for use; and without which it would be of comparatively little value. They partake somewhat of the nature of the investments which manufacturers are compelled to make, from time to time, in improved machinery for the purpose of rendering their capital more productive. The existence of such conveniences, paid for out of the public rates, increases the amount of rent received by the landlords. Moreover, local rates do not fall wholly upon the land, but partially upon the occupiers. In the long run, it is true, the incidence of such burdens is upon the property itself, but every increase falls in the first instance upon the tenant, and if it be merely temporary, upon him exclusively; if it become permanent, it affects the amount of rent which the landlord would otherwise have received upon the renewal of a tenancy. According to the ordinary arguments frequently employed upon the subject, it might be supposed that the landlord actually pays the local rates out of his rental, or, in other words, out of the net sum which he receives from the tenant after the latter has paid the local rates. If this were true, they would be paid twice over; it is, however, quite contrary to the actual fact.

The obvious argument against any inequality in the assessment of real and personal property to this tax, is the fact that the value of the former is based upon the net income received by the landowner; local rates are excluded from the calculation. As Mr. John Stuart Mill has clearly shown, they become a rent charge upon the property in favour of the State;* upon the capital which the local burdens represent no duty of any kind is paid; they form an element in calculating the amount of rent to be paid to the

---

* Principles of Political Economy. Book V., c. ii., secs. 5, 6. See Note to sec. 6.

landlord, but not in calculating the capitalised value of that rent. The recipient of a legacy of £10,000 in land occupies an exactly similar position to the recipient of £10,000 in money, as far as local burdens are concerned; there is, however, this great distinction in favour of the former, his investment is the most sure and stable that it is possible to conceive. He has comparatively little care or anxiety, he may quietly fold his arms, and will still receive the increasing rent which a prosperous and active community will pour into his coffers. The recipient of £10,000 in capital must look well to the security of his investments; if he employs it in trade or manufactures he must diligently and carefully devote himself to the management of his business. "The ordinary progress of a society," says Mr. John Stuart Mill, "which increases in wealth, is at all times tending to augment the incomes of landlords; to give them both a greater amount and a greater proportion of the wealth of the community, independently of any trouble or outlay incurred by themselves. They grow richer, as it were, in their sleep, without working, risking, or economizing. What claim have they, on the general principles of social justice, to this accession of riches?" Mr. Mill raises a broad question, into which it is unnecessary to enter at present; the facts upon which he bases his arguments are, however, indisputable; the taxpaying public may, therefore, fairly ask, what claim have the owners of the land to the exemption from taxation, which they now enjoy under the Act which levies the succession duties?

The most obvious reply appears to be, that the duty, as now imposed, was all that the Government of 1853 felt themselves able to carry; it was a compromise which secured an instalment of justice, not its perfect triumph.

It is true that Mr. Dudley Baxter questions the soundness of Mr. Mill's argument;* and endeavours to illustrate the case by examples taken from commercial transactions. There is, however, this great distinction between landed and other kinds of property. The value of the former increases, as Mr Mill observes, " without exertion or sacrifice on the part of the owners, but with complete passiveness on their part." The merchant who buys a cargo of tea, or stores a large quantity of corn is not passive; the profit he receives is the result of his active enterprise. Mr. Mill's argument is simply this, the enterprise of the merchant and trader, the industry and skill of the manufacturer, farmer, mechanic, and labourer increase the value of real property, without any effort on the part of the landlord. What right has the latter to reap exclusively the results of such enterprise? Mr. Baxter asks, has the State a right to the increased value of land in a town which a capitalist has purchased in order to reap the profits of such increase when required for building? No question could possibly arise on this point were the condition of such special taxation understood at the time of purchase; it is solely

---

* The Taxation of the United Kingdom, 1869, pp. 50—58,

because the sound principle advocated by Mr. Mill has not been law that any difficulty exists. He has, however, carefully guarded his argument against the charge of injustice, by an explanation of the mode in which he would practically carry out his proposal. Mr. Baxter asks, if a landlord makes a road or railway through his property, is that a case in which the State should claim the increased value thus created? In such a case the increase is created by the enterprise of the landowner—it is not the spontaneous increase of which Mr. Mill writes. There is, without doubt, a great evil in our system of local rating, in the fact that no measures have been adopted to reach the excessive ground rents, which are a legitimate subject of taxation. The greatest pressure has been thereby thrown, in times of distress, upon those least able to bear it, while the revenues of wealthy ground landlords have been comparatively untouched.

A suggestion was made by Mr. Newmarch, at a recent meeting of the Statistical Society, that an equivalent for the succession duty should be levied upon all property held by Corporations. This is manifestly an equitable proposition; the tax is levied upon property; it is paid in return for the protection afforded by the State. If property, which otherwise would be subject to this tax, escapes in consequence of its being held by a body which being perpetual has no successors, a heavier burden is thrown upon all other property in consequence of this exemption. If " the exemption of one man means the extra taxation of another," as asserted by Mr. Gladstone, in his Financial Statement for 1853, it is equally true that the exemption of one class of property means the extra taxation of all other property. The same argument applies to the taxation of property held by charities. Exemption in that case involves a compulsory contribution from the remainder of the community, which should be done, if desirable, by a direct vote of the House of Commons.

Objections have been raised that these duties are paid out of capital, that they are therefore fines upon industry, and discourage accumulation. It does not appear, however, that they have exercised any serious influence in this direction. It has been already shown in the case of real estate, that during a series of years the tendency of value is almost invariably upwards; the succession duty may therefore be justly regarded as a deferred payment of taxation. During the life of the owner he has been allowed to retain a portion of his rental, which otherwise would have been received yearly by the State. It is clear that this may, if he choose, be invested and the payment of the succession duty thus provided for. In that happy period when a perfect system of taxation shall have been devised, it may be possible to dispense with legacy and succession duties; at present they seem to be almost indispensable. They are not by any means, the most injurious portion of our fiscal system; they press upon industry with far less weight than duties of Customs and Excise, taxes on locomotion, or Licenses upon trade and manufactures. If confined to a moderate rate, and levied fairly and equitably on all sorts of property they are less objectionable than many other taxes.

CHAPTER XIII.

MISCELLANEOUS STAMP DUTIES.

A very wide range of taxation is comprised under the head of Stamps. It has been already seen that several licenses on trades and professions, some taxes on commodities, and the legacy and succession duties are collected in this manner. The remaining stamp duties are enumerated in Sir Thomas Bazley's return under the following heads:—*

	Number	£	s.
Deeds and other Instruments not otherwise enumerated	...	1,586,809	7
Bills of Exchange, Inland	6,112,589	381,633	3
" Foreign	277,478	324,048	16
Bankers' Notes and Composition for Bankers' Bills and Notes	...	131,714	0
Receipts and Drafts, and other documents	142,011,810	591,810	17
Marine Insurances	No account kept.	85,960	9
Newspaper Stamps	26,908,115	115,987	19
Probate Court Fee Stamps	377,084	136,584	15
Admiralty Court Fee Stamps	21,900	8,686	10
Divorce and Matrimonial Causes Fee Stamps (England)	13,811	2,836	15
Patents for Inventions	101,742	119,380	1

---

* Parliamentary Paper, "Taxes and Imposts," Sess. 1869. No. 427.

	Number.	£	s.
Land Registry Fee Stamps, England	4,147	1,501	10
Common Law Court Fee Stamps	694,840	91,775	6
Companies Registration Fee Stamps	13,968	7,516	18
Registration of Deeds Fee Stamps, Ireland	49,106	10,873	1
Record of Title Fee Stamps, Ireland	217	63	5
Chancery Fee Fund Stamps	76,711	15,600	14
Law, Chancery, Judgments Registry, and Civil Bill Funds, Ireland	623,274	30,542	18
Copyhold, Inclosure, and Tithe Commission Fee Stamps	1,397	1,620	0
Public Record Fee Stamps	3,053	590	10

The collection of Stamp Duties is rendered comparatively easy from the circumstance that payment of the duty is generally necessary to ensure the affixing of the stamp which renders the document valid. The principle upon which they were originally based was, that all documents requiring stamps were to be written on parchment or paper already stamped. In practice this was found inconvenient, and especially so, as in some instances it was almost impossible to decide what amount of duty was payable. The complexity of the Stamp duties, previously to recent alterations, was such that expensive litigation was frequently caused owing to the insufficiency of stamps used even in cases in which they had been adopted under legal advice. In alluding to this evil Mr. Mc Culloch said of these duties, in 1845;*—" one would think they had been

---

* Treatise on Taxation, pp. 276—7.

intended to serve as decoys with which to entrap parties, and force them into the courts; the difficulty which they create of determining what is and what is not a proper stamp is itself a most prolific source of uncertainty, and consequently of litigation and expense."

It was impossible that evils such as are thus desscribed should escape attention during a period in which successive revisions of taxation have taken place. Accordingly these duties have been materially modified since 1849; in many instances they have been largely reduced, and thus rendered more tolerable to the taxpayer. The most notable example was the reduction of the stamp upon receipts to a uniform duty of one penny, in place of rates varying from 3d. to 10s. It is a well-known fact that payment of this duty was very largely evaded before the introduction of the penny stamp. In commercial transactions the law was almost a dead letter, stamps being hardly ever employed unless demanded by the payer, and even then the requirement of a stamped receipt was held to be a reflection upon the honesty of the person receiving the money. The introduction of the uniform penny receipt worked an entire change; the modest request of a penny was readily complied with, and the use of stamped receipts became general. The result of this measure in securing the due collection of the duty is shown in the amount collected before and after the reduction, which took place in 1853.*

---

* First Inland Revenue Report, 1857. App. p. xcix.

	Before Reduction.		After Reduction.
	£		£
1851	187,876	1854	245,367
1852	194,088	1855	281,845

The increase of the first complete year, under the new system, over the last complete year of the old, was £51,279.

Taxes upon the sale and transfer of property are considered objectionable by political economists, because they are levied upon transactions which are beneficial to the community. There is also another objection, that they fall mainly upon one description of property. It is true that, according to the words of the Statute, the duties are levied upon the conveyance of property real or personal, but as the bulk of personal property requires no written conveyance the incidence of the duty is mainly upon real estate. It is difficult to allege a reason why a transfer of land should be subject to a tax, while a transfer of iron, cotton, or any similar article is untaxed, unless there be a special service rendered by the State in the case of the first named transaction. If stamp duties upon the sale of property gave increased security to such transactions, they would possess a compensating feature which would render them a more equitable means of raising a portion of the national revenue than they are at present. Upon this point the following remarks by Mr. McCulloch are deserving attention:—*

"A tax on the transfer of property should bear a uniform proportion to the value of the property trans-

---

* Treatise on Taxation, pp. 275-6.

ferred; and the burden which it imposes should be, in part at least, compensated by assessing the tax so as to facilitate and authenticate the transactions on which it is charged, and to render them less hazardous to the parties concerned. The mode of levying this tax resorted to in many countries of Europe, where it is imposed on registration, under a system adapted to facilitate the proofs of transfer, and to guard against fraudulent conveyances, seems to secure these advantages, and to be the best hitherto suggested."

In addition to stamps on conveyances, the duties collected under the head of "deeds and other instruments not otherwise enumerated" include stamps on admission of Barristers, Attorneys, and Physicians; articles of clerkship; indentures of apprenticeship; agreements, leases, awards, bonds; collation to ecclesiastical benefices, dignities or promotions; commissions in the Army, Navy, and other offices; registration of public companies; delivery orders, dock warrants; grants of letters patent under the Great Seal of honours, dignities and offices; mortgages, power of attorney, and several other duties. It is quite impossible to enter into a detailed examination of these numerous duties within the limits of this work. Collected under the authority of various Acts of Parliament, beginning with the reign of William and Mary, and regulated by numerous decisions of the Courts of Law, the Stamp duties are a code of laws in themselves, requiring a special technical treatise for their interpretation. Long use has accustomed the public to these payments, and although they may be indefensible upon purely abstract grounds, they raise a considerable revenue in a mode to which apparently the public does not entertain any serious objection, and, except in some special cases, where the duties are paid by solicitors at the Stamp Office, and attendances for that purpose are charged to their clients, at a moderate cost compared with the heavy burden involved in taxes upon commodities.

The convenience of stamps as instruments for the payment of fees in Courts of Law, especially the security they afford for the due payment of such fees into the Treasury, have led to their employment for that purpose. Taxes upon law proceedings are generally condemned by political economists, on the ground that they are an impediment to the obtaining of justice. Heavy taxes upon the administration of the law are, without doubt, objectionable, but moderate fees payable during the various stages of legal proceedings cannot be said to produce any serious evil, but rather to check unnecessary litigation. In this way the cost is divided between the general public and the parties more immediately interested in the actions tried in Courts of Law. If litigation were to be had perfectly free of charge it is very questionable whether the remedy would not, in many cases, be worse than the disease. At the rates now paid these fees form a very small proportion of the costs of a suit either in law or equity, and can hardly be said to hinder the course of justice.

A much more serious objection may be urged against the duty on Marine Insurances, which, like the Fire Insurance Duty just repealed, is a tax imposed upon prudence. It falls mainly upon the smaller owners, large capitalists being able to insure their own ships. It is a remnant of the fiscal system which seized upon every available transaction for the purpose of obtaining taxes for the government, and is utterly indefensible upon any principle of taxation, recognised by any system of sound political economy. If a tax on shipping is advisable it should be universal in its incidence, and not, as at present, levied exclusively upon prudent men who seek to protect themselves against the possibility of loss from causes over which they have no control.

There may be some show of reason for a tax upon shipping, on the ground that a considerable portion of our naval expenditure is incurred for its special protection, but none for a tax specially levied upon its insurance against the elements. A tax on shipping would, however, be paid by the consumer, and would enhance the price of commodities; it would be quite as reasonable to tax railway trucks.

The Stamp Duties on Patents of Invention are open to similar objections, if levied at a rate more than sufficient to defray the expenses of registration. The inventor of a new process is a public benefactor; it is, therefore, impolitic for the State to impose a tax in consequence of his having exercised his talent in the public service. The existing law of patents was framed for the purpose of enabling inventors to reap the profit of their inventions; in return they may be fairly expected to contribute a sum adequate to the maintenance of the Patent Office, to which purpose the fees payable upon the granting of patents ought to be strictly limited.

CHAPTER XIV.

TAXES ON RAILWAYS, SERVANTS, CARRIAGES, HORSES, MULES, DOGS, AND ARMORIAL BEARINGS.

The only special tax now remaining on locomotion is the railway passenger duty, which is assessed at 5 per cent. on all sums received for conveyance of passengers, excepting such as are conveyed, in compliance with the terms of the Railway Act, at one penny per mile. It produced, during the last financial year, the sum of £500,383 3s. on £10,007,667.*

The taxes on locomotion repealed, by the Act 32 & 33 Vic., cap. 14, from the 1st of January, 1869, are the following:—

	Amount for year 1868-9.†		
	£	s.	d.
Stage Carriage Duty	36,274	2	0
Hackney Carriage Duty	100,050	4	0
Post Horse License Duty	142,196	3	0
Stage Carriage Licenses	6,524	3	0
Hackney Carriage Licenses (London)	6,109	0	0

It is difficult to understand why the duty on railway passengers should remain, when similar imposts have

---

* Parliamentary Return, Session 1867, No. 427.   † Ibid.

been repealed. The only valid reason that can be assigned, is the want of a sufficient surplus to ensure its removal. Railway Companies are assessed to the income tax, railway stock pays probate and legacy duties, railways contribute to local taxation; it would seem, therefore, that they are adequately taxed without any special payment being imposed upon them. In some cases they meet with competition from steam boats, which, in addition to the advantage of having no permanent way to provide for, pay no passenger duty. It may, however, be expected from the observations of the Chancellor of the Exchequer, in his Budget speech for 1869, that at an early period this tax will also follow the other recently repealed taxes on locomotion, and disappear from our fiscal system. The taxes on horses, carriages, and dogs were formerly collected as Assessed Taxes. In 1867 the tax on dogs was changed from an assessed tax to an excise license, and the duty reduced from 12s. to 5s. each. At the same time, the exemption in favour of dogs used in tending or driving sheep and cattle was abolished, and the collection of the duty removed from the hands of persons appointed by District Commissioners to those of the officers of the Excise. The effect of this change was seen in the increased number of dogs charged with duty. The number assessed in Great Britain during the year ending 5th April, 1866, was 394,837; while the number of dog licenses granted between the 1st April and the 15th November, 1867, was 817,970; showing an increase of above 400,000 dogs licensed in eight months of 1867, above the number returned to the Assessed Taxes during the whole of the preceding year. The number of licenses granted during the year ending 31st March, 1869, was 1,068,221, and the amount of revenue £267,055. "It is evident from these figures," say the Inland Revenue Commissioners, "that the 'local knowledge' of the parochial assessors, on which so much reliance is placed, has failed to discover the existence of many hundred thousand dogs which the new system of collection has at once brought into charge."*

The success of this measure led to the introduction by Mr. Lowe of a similar change in the collection of the duties on servants, carriages, horses, and armorial bearings. By the Customs and Inland Revenue Act, passed on the 24th June, 1869, the assessed duties levied in respect of male servants, carriages, horses, mares, geldings, mules, hair powder, and armorial bearings were repealed after the 5th of April, 1869, in England, and the 24th of May, 1869, in Scotland. In lieu thereof, the following Excise Licences were imposed from the 1st of January, 1870:—

	£	s.	d.
For every Male Servant	0	15	0
For every Carriage— If such Carriage shall have four or more wheels, and shall be of the weight of four hundredweight, or upwards	2	2	0

---

* Eleventh Inland Revenue Report, 1867, pp. 13, 14, 15.

	£	s.	d.
If such Carriage shall have less than four wheels, or having four or more wheels, shall be of a less weight than four hundredweight	0	15	0
For every Horse or Mule	0	10	6
For Armorial Bearings—			
If such Armorial Bearings shall be painted, marked, or affixed on or to any Carriage	2	2	0
If such Armorial Bearings shall not be so painted, marked, or affixed, but shall be otherwise worn or used	1	1	0

The duties for which this simple table is substituted were thirty-two in number, assessed at various rates. The assessed taxes on carriages let for hire have been increased by the measure, but this is more than compensated by the removal of the license duty on post horses and stage carriages. One great merit of the measure is the mode in which it has simplified the law respecting these taxes. By the Customs and Inland Revenue Act of the Session of 1869, thirty-two Acts of Parliament relating to assessed and excise duties are wholly, and twenty are partially, repealed. Eleven of these Acts were passed in the reign of George III., ten in that of George IV., thirteen in that of William IV., and eighteen during the reign of her present Majesty. The law relating to duties upon male servants, carriages, horses, and armorial bearings is now comprised in twenty sections of an Act of Parliament; the excise licenses are made payable during the month of January in each year, and a declaration is required from every person liable to pay them, giving full particulars as to his liability. Provisions are also made to secure the revenue against fraudulent returns, and for the infliction of penalties upon defaulters who have not made the necessary returns.

Horses used solely in husbandry and in underground mines and mares kept for breeding purposes are exempt from duty. It is a curious anomaly that the owners of horses engaged in agriculture should be exempt from a tax which the owners of horses engaged in the delivery of agricultural produce to the consumer are compelled to pay; there is no valid reason for any special exemption from this tax. It is no doubt intended that these duties should fall mainly upon the wealthy; but in many instances owners of horses are taxed whose living depends upon hard work, and who are quite as deserving of relief from such a burden upon their trade as the agriculturists of Great Britain. The inconsistencies and inequalities of the Assessed Taxes are a valid argument against them. It is difficult to know why male servants alone should be taxed, or why a tradesman who employs his errand boy to clean knives and shoes should pay a tax for him as a servant. It is equally difficult to understand why a waiter at an hotel should be charged, while assistants in a retail shop escape. All taxes on employment are bad taxes; it is quite impossible to assess them in a way which shall cause them to operate, as evidently intended, as taxes upon wealth. The changes of last year have no doubt simplified these imposts, but have not removed the fundamental objection to such a method of taxation. They have one advantage as contrasted with some portions of our fiscal system; being paid directly, they do not take more from the taxpayer than is received by the Government, in other respects they are quite as objectionable as duties of customs and excise upon commodities.

CHAPTER XV.

INHABITED HOUSE DUTY.

The present house tax was substituted in 1851 for the duty previously assessed on windows. The Inland Revenue Commissioners estimate the amount of relief to the taxpayer afforded by this measure to be represented by an actual loss to the revenue of about £1,000,000: the window duty in 1850 having produced £1,708,504, and the house duty having varied from £693,736 to £728,969.* The amount produced during the financial year ending March 31, 1869, was £1,131,582 10s., being a considerable increase since 1857, but still not equal in amount to the produce of the window duty in 1850.†

The gross amount of the assessment was as follows:

	Duty.	Annual Value Assessed. £
Shops and warehouses partially occupied as dwellings	6d. in £	8,049,332
Beer-shops	6d. in £	3,118,229
Farm-houses	6d. in £	629,143
Dwelling-houses	9d. in £	23,267,149

---

* First Inland Revenue Report, 1857, p. 35.
† Parliamentary Paper, Sess. 1869. No. 427.

The relief to the taxpayer arising from the substitution of this tax for the window duty, which was £1,000,000 in 1857, is now fully £1,500,000, owing to the increased number of houses which, but for that change, would have been subject to the heavier burden of the window duty.

The following are the words of the Act of Parliament granting these duties:—" For every inhabited dwelling-house which, with the household and other offices, yards, and gardens therewith occupied and charged, is or shall be worth the rent of £20 or upwards by the year; where any such dwelling-house shall be occupied by any person in trade who shall expose to sale and sell any goods, wares, or merchandise in any shop or warehouse, being part of the same dwelling-house, and in the front and on the ground or basement story thereof; and also where any such dwelling-house shall be occupied by any person who shall be duly licensed by the laws in force to sell therein by retail beer, ale, wine or other liquors, although the room or rooms thereof in which any such liquors shall be exposed to sale, sold, drunk or consumed shall not be such shop or warehouse as aforesaid; and also where any such dwelling-house shall be a farm-house occupied by a tenant or farm servant, and *bonâ fide* used for the purposes of husbandry only, there shall be charged for every 20s. of such annual value of any such dwelling-house the sum of 6d. And where any such dwelling-house shall not be occupied and used for any such purpose and in manner aforesaid, there shall be charged for every 20s. of such annual value thereof the sum of 9d."*

A Tax on Houses was, for a very long period, a part of the ordinary revenue of Great Britain. It was first imposed in 1696, during the reign of William the Third, and continued uninterruptedly till the year 1834, when it was repealed. A tax on windows was imposed at the same time; at first it formed a supplementary house duty, but in 1747 it became a separate tax and continued in existence until the year 1851.† A tax on windows is much more objectionable on many accounts than a tax on houses. The number of windows in a house is no criterion of its value, or of the means of the occupier; the rent paid for a house, on the contrary, generally bears a fixed proportion to the income of the occupier. The imposition of the tax on windows interfered seriously with the health and comfort of the people. It led to the construction of houses upon imperfect principles in respect to the two great essentials of light and ventilation; the number of windows being generally regulated, not according to the necessities of the occupants, but in order to evade, as far as possible, the window duty. The commutation of this obnoxious impost into the tax now levied upon dwellings was almost universally regarded as a great boon, at the time when the change was made, and

---

* 14 and 15 Vic., c. 36.

† First Inland Revenue Report, 1857. App. p. cliii. Act 14 and 15 Vic. cap. 36, sec. 1.

there can be no question that it has added very largely to the public comfort, convenience, and health.

The houses subject to this tax are inhabited dwelling-houses; warehouses, and places entirely occupied for business purposes, being exempt from duty. It operates with hardship in some instances: the tradesman who lives in a highly rented house for the purposes of his trade is assessed at sixpence in the pound, while the physician, to whom a good situation is equally important, has to pay the full rate of ninepence. It has been decided by the judges that a house occupied by a carpenter and builder, part of which was employed as a counting-house and workshops, is liable to the ninepenny rate.* The same decision was given in the case of an eating-house and coffee-shop, although cooked meat was exposed in the shop window on the ground floor.† These are inequalities in the assessment of the tax, which ought to be removed by legislation; if the differential rate in favour of houses partly occupied for trade purposes is continued, it should be equally and fairly applied.

The House Tax is regarded as an equitable tax by most writers on the subject of Taxation. Mr. John Stuart Mill, in the Principles of Political Economy,‡ enters at some length into the question of its incidence, and the conclusion at which he arrives is

---

* Fourth Inland Revenue Report, 1860, App. p. 25.

† Ibid. 1861, App. p. 57.

‡ Book 5, c. iii. sec. 6.

that " a house-tax, if justly proportioned to the value of the house, is one of the fairest and most unobjectionable of all taxes. No part of a person's expenditure is a better criterion of his means, or bears, on the whole, more nearly the same proportion to them." Mr. McCulloch,* writing soon after the repeal of the House Tax, in 1834, says :—" We cannot help regarding the abolition of the late house-tax as an ill-advised concession to vulgar and unfounded clamour. A tax on houses interferes with no department or branch of industry; the subject on which the tax is laid is obvious, and cannot be concealed; and it is never any very difficult matter to determine the value of houses with sufficient precision for its fair assessment." He also says, " when these taxes are assessed according to the rent they are among the least exceptional that can be devised."

" The rent of a house," says Adam Smith,† " may be distinguished into two parts, of which the one may very properly be called the building rent, the other is commonly called the ground rent." This division of rent is an unquestionable fact, and it therefore follows that a tax on the rent of a house is partly a tax on the land upon which it stands, and partly a tax on the house itself. The proportion which the ground rent and the house rent bear to each other depends entirely upon the situation of the house. In many parts of

---

* Treatise on Taxation, 1846, p. 70.

† Wealth of Nations, Book 5 c. 2.

the country a dwelling house may be obtained at a rent of twenty pounds, for which forty, fifty, or even sixty would be paid in London and some of the larger cities and towns. The difference is not in the amount of rent paid for the building, but in the value of the ground on which it stands.

That portion of the rent which is paid for the house itself is regulated by the amount necessary to provide for the interest upon the capital expended in its construction, for repairs, and for the ordinary trade profits of the builder. If the demand for houses is great and rents are increased, fresh capital is attracted into the business of providing dwelling houses; if, on the other hand, the demand is less than the supply, rents decrease, and capital seeks more profitable channels for investment. In this, as in other avocations, the rate of profit cannot long remain higher than the average of general trade profits. In considering the question of the incidence of this portion of the house tax, these facts must not be lost sight of; the profits of the owner of the building being regulated by the current rate of trade profits, it appears that the portion of the tax, which appertains to the building itself, falls upon the occupier.

It has been already shown that the respective proportions of ground and building rents vary according to locality. In villages and smaller towns where land is plentiful, ground rent forms a very inconsiderable portion of the gross amount. In larger towns and the metropolis, especially in peculiar situations, it frequently forms the larger proportion. On no other principle can widely different rents for the same class of buildings be explained. In cases where the higher rents are paid the larger proportion of the house tax is not a tax upon the house, but upon the land on which it stands, and, although paid by the occupier, ultimately falls upon the owner. It may be true, as urged by Mr. Mill, that in the case of the lowest rates of ground rents, which are but a trifle above the rents obtained for agricultural purposes, the incidence of the tax is affected by the circumstance that, as land becomes more valuable for building than for cultivation, fresh land is brought into the market. This process is not, however, capable of indefinite extension; as towns and cities increase in size, land in the centre of them becomes more and more valuable the supply being limited, and owners of the soil enjoy a monopoly, by means of which they obtain excessive rents. The amount which occupiers are able to pay is represented by the rent *plus* the tax; if the latter were repealed it may fairly be presumed that, upon the termination of existing holdings, the entire benefit would be absorbed by the landlord, the relief to the occupier would be but temporary. In the case of all leases entered upon since the imposition of the house tax in 1851 there can be no doubt that its amount, as well as the local rates, was an element in the consideration of the rent to be paid; while, in the case of all leases dated before that period, there has been a considerable relief from taxation by the substitution of this duty for the more burdensome tax on windows. The repeal of the house tax, in so far as it is a tax upon the high ground rents of large towns, would simply bestow a bonus upon the landed proprietors at the expense of the rest of the community.

This opinion appears to be fully corroborated by the information received in answer to enquiries made by Mr. Dudley Baxter, during the preparation of his recent work on Taxation.* Speaking of local rates which are levied upon the same principle as the House Tax, he says:—"Many practical men concur with me in thinking that the average incidence of rates is three-fourths on the landlord, and one-fourth on the tenant." If this be the case, and there does not appear any reason to doubt the accuracy of his conclusion, it appears that the amount of relief that would accrue to the occupiers of Great Britain by the repeal of the House Tax, would be £282,895. It has been already shown that, so far as the building is concerned, profits are not affected by the tax, so that the sum of £848,687, being the difference between the full amount produced by the tax and the portion paid by the occupier, would, after a shorter or longer interval, according to the duration of the present occupancy, be simply transferred from the State to the owners of the property.

It has been recently urged as a complaint against this tax, that it imposes injurious and unnecessary restrictions upon the erection of dwellings for the working classes. It is difficult to see how this can

---

* The Taxation of the United Kingdom, pp. 59-67.

be the case, inasmuch as all houses under £20 rental are exempt. It will no doubt be said that in London, owing to the high ground rents, workmen are compelled to reside in unfurnished lodgings, and that the houses thus let out, being beyond the value of £20, are assessed to the House Tax. That fact may be an argument in favour of remitting the tax upon houses thus occupied by the working classes, but would not justify its entire repeal. It cannot, however, be seriously maintained that the tax places any injurious restrictions upon workmen's dwellings, if they are rightly constructed. It is true that houses of the value of £20 are taxed, but if houses for the working classes are built in flats, so as to bring the rent of each separate occupation under £20, they are not subject to the tax. It is only when the present pernicious system of crowding several families into a single house is followed, that the working-man is subject to the House Tax. Moreover, it is not the tax that is the difficulty, but the value of the land; unless that can be reduced, the removal of the House Tax will afford but small facility for the erection of workmen's dwellings. As far as this tax is a tax upon ground rents, no relief would be afforded to the working classes by its removal; the whole benefit would be absorbed by the landlord. It is merely in respect of that portion which falls upon building rent, that they would derive any advantage. The difficulty, as far as working-men are concerned, would be met by adopting Mr. Mill's proposal to value and assess separately every portion of a house which is occupied by a separate tenant, as is now usually the case with chambers.

Another ground of objection is that it presses very unequally upon different classes of the community, and falls most heavily upon persons of moderate means. If all taxes which offend in these respects are to be proscribed, the Chancellor of the Exchequer has before him the arduous task of inventing an entirely new system of taxation. The income tax falls most heavily on persons of moderate means; so do duties of Customs and Excise. If ten per cent. is taken by taxation from an income of £200, it falls upon that income far more heavily than a tax of ten per cent. upon £2,000. This is an evil which is not peculiar to the house tax, and, unless a graduated scale of taxation be adopted, taking a larger proportion from large incomes than from small ones, it is impossible to remedy this grievance. At all events it is hardly fair to charge as a peculiar hardship in the case of the house tax, an imperfection which it shares in common with all other taxes.

Whatever may be urged against a tax upon houses, there can be no question that a tax on ground rents is a legitimate source from which to derive a portion of the national revenue, and it has been shown that in the larger towns this tax is, in a great degree, a tax on ground rents, and to that extent is quite unobjectionable. The house tax does not interfere with building, it imposes no burdens upon trade or manufactures, it is paid directly to the State, and involves no extra charges upon the taxpayer. It is assessed upon that portion of his income which he feels that he can afford to spend, and thus leaves his savings untouched. In all these respects it possesses great advantages as compared with many other existing taxes, and until more serious burdens upon trade, manufactures, and employment have been removed, it would be a great pity to part with a source of revenue to which so little exception can be taken.

CHAPTER XVI.

THE LAND TAX.

This tax is the sole surviving fragment of that portion of the ancient constitution of England, which imposed the duty of providing for the defence of the realm upon the holders of landed estate. During the feudal ages all the lands of the country were held either directly or indirectly from the Crown, in consideration of certain services to be rendered, and of certain payments to be made by the tenants. For a very long period the main portion of the revenue of the country was derived from the land. Customs duties were but small and unproductive, and the Excise was unknown, prior to its imposition by the Long Parliament. Mr. Mc Culloch says :* " during the feudal system the obligation of military service, with the different payments to the sovereign, under the heads of aids, reliefs, fines on alienation, purveyance, wardship, primer-seisin, scutages, hydages, escheats, and so forth, due by the proprietors of estates held directly of the Crown (who

---

* Principles of Taxation, 1815, pp. 56-57.

in their turn exacted similar payments from their sub-tenants), fell wholly on the land, and were, in effect, so many land taxes. These revenues, added to the rental of the Crown estates, were for a considerable period adequate to defray the expenses of government."

The transfer of these burdens from the landowners to the people was accompanied by another change in the long established policy of the realm, the introduction of a standing army. In Saxon times, the Militia, which was established by king Alfred, made all the people soldiers. During the feudal ages standing armies were unknown. In addition to the feudal services of the holders of land the people were trained to the use of arms, and the defence of the kingdom was entrusted to their care. Upon the restoration of Charles the Second an entirely new system was inaugurated. The army, which during the troubled period of the Commonwealth had become a power in the State, was made a permanent institution, the landholders relieved themselves from their feudal obligations, and in lieu thereof settled one-half the excise upon the king and his heirs for ever. The civil war paved the way for this change; during its continuance each party was compelled to raise a force, irrespective of the old conditions of knight service, and new modes of raising a revenue were required. These consisted mainly of taxes on real and personal property and the excise. It appears, from the best information that can be obtained, that the total amount raised in England during the period of the Commonwealth was above £83,000,000, or about £4,300,000 annually, half of which was obtained by various contributions from the land.*

At the restoration of Charles the Second all the feudal prerogatives of the Sovereign were restored also; but the great landowners embraced the opportunity, afforded by the necessity of providing a revenue for the Crown, to make a fundamental change in their tenures, and thus relieved themselves from the obligations under which they had previously held their estates, throwing the burden upon the people in the shape of duties of excise. The measure, however, met with considerable opposition, many members of Parliament speaking strongly against the excise, and in favour of a tax upon the land. Ultimately it was resolved, by a majority of 2, the numbers being for the resolution 151, and against it 149, "that the moiety of the excise of beer, ale, cyder, perry, and strong waters, at the rate it was now levied, shall be settled on the King's majesty, his heirs and successors, in full recompense and satisfaction for all tenures *in capite*, and by knight service; and of the Court of wards and liveries; and all emoluments thereby accruing, and in full satisfaction of all purveyance."†

This resolution was carried into effect by the Act

---

* The Constitutional Right to a Revision of Land Tax, Ridgway, 1842, pp. 22, 23.

† Ibid., pp. 25—26.

12 Chas. II, cap. 24, which is described by Blackstone as a greater acquisition to the property of the Kingdom than even Magna Charta itself, inasmuch as the latter only pruned the luxuriances, which had grown out of military tenures, whereas this statute exterpated them root and branch.* There can be very little doubt that the feudal prerogatives of the Crown had been frequently exercised in a very oppressive manner, and with little regard to the actual rights of the parties. The system, however admirably it might have been adapted for a feudal era, was, no doubt, out of place as another phase of society was gradually developed. Relief from the uncertainties and vexations of feudal obligations was a special and peculiar advantage to the landlords. The grievances abolished directly affected them only, and in justice the substitute provided ought to have been a tax on land, as advocated by the minority of 149. Such an arrangement would have been a great advantage to the landowners, while it would have imposed no fresh burdens upon the people. The course adopted, in preference to this simple and honest commutation of previous obligations, laid the foundation of a fiscal policy, which proved not only most disastrous for the public, but highly disadvantageous for the very class in whose supposed interest it was framed. Excise Duties then first permanently levied, were afterwards increased and multiplied to such an extent, that at

---

* Stephen's Commentaries on the Laws of England, Book 2, part 1, chap. 2, 1858, p. 205.

length, in conjunction with an elaborate and protective customs tariff, they nearly annihilated the productive industry of the country. Agriculture was for a very long period in a condition of chronic distress, and there can be little doubt that the rents received by the landlords, during the period of heavy duties, were far smaller than they would have been if the industry of the country had been left free from the trammels of customs and excise.

Another most important change then introduced, was the conversion of the landholders into landowners. By the feudal system the land of the country was vested in the Crown as the representative of the community. It was held by the great landholders, subject to the performance of certain duties and the payment of certain taxes. It was the means by which the Sovereign obtained soldiers for the conduct of his wars. The change in the tenure of land, effected in 1660, is described, in a work previously referred to,* as one which " completely altered the fundamental element of the constitution of this country. The Government of England previously to that Act was a feudal monarchy, the very essence of which is, that the public expenses of the Government, both in war and peace, shall be defrayed by the various feudatories, the deficiency, if any, being provided for out of the public property in land vested in the monarch for the time being, and by taxes or subsidies granted by Parliament, and levied on the land and personal property

---

* The Constitutional Right to a Revision of the Land Tax, pp. 28-29.

of the kingdom. This Act gave to the feudatories of England a complete discharge, as the lawyers are in the habit of very correctly wording it, from the oppressive fruits and incidents of their tenure. It confirmed to them their rights, discharged from the correlative obligations; and thus created the moral and legal anomaly of rights without obligations—an anomaly which cannot exist without a legal and logical absurdity, and a moral fraud." From the passing of that Act the property of the nation in the soil was transferred to a section of the community. Another serious evil followed this injustice; the privilege of Government became divorced from the responsibility of providing the ways and means of its administration and the cost of the wars, in which the Sovereign and his advisers might involve the nation. So long as the obligations of the military tenures existed, the landholders had a direct interest, both in checking needless wars, and in bringing such as were undertaken to a speedy termination. The modern system having placed the burden upon the shoulders of the people, who were unrepresented in Parliament, the direct incentive to frugality, which the sense of personal responsibility for expenditure provided, was removed. It was this circumstance which rendered it possible for the rulers of this country to involve the nation in long and costly Continental wars, for objects in which the interests of the people were but little concerned. The so-called balance of power might be a question of great importance to the ruling classes, but it was one of little moment to the masses of the population, who were far more deeply interested in good government at home, than in the questionable proceedings of the notorious Holy Alliance. The sole result of these wars, so far as the great mass of the people of this country were concerned, was an intolerable addition to the burdens imposed upon trade and industry, and the imposition of restraints upon personal and political freedom, from which the nation is not even yet entirely free.

It has been already seen that during the period of the Commonwealth a considerable portion of the revenue was raised by assessments on real and personal property, levied according to the public exigencies. As the sum of £1,200,000 a year fixed for the ordinary revenue of Charles II. was insufficient to provide for all his expenses, the assessment of property, established during the Commonwealth, was continued to supply the deficiency.

The following table shows the various items of the revenue and the average annual receipt during the reigns of Charles II. and James II. :—*

	Charles II. £	James II. £
Crown lands	105,000	
Land tax	500,000	100,000
Customs	400,000	1,015,472
Excise	294,950	676,387
Miscellaneous	386,760	310,000
Total	£1,686,710	£2,101,859

* The Constitutional Right to a Revision of the Land Tax, p.p. 56-57.

It appears from these figures that the annual sum received from duties of Customs and Excise, during the reign of James II., was considerably more than double the amount raised in that manner during the reign of his brother. The amount derived annually from the tax on property was, however, but one-fifth of that which had been paid during the reign of Charles II. In fact the land-owners refused to grant more than one aid of £400,000 from that source. The burden thus thrown upon the people gave rise to serious complaints, and it was one of the promises held out by the friends of William III. that there should be a reduction and re-adjustment of taxation. Accordingly one of the first Acts of the Convention Parliament, which met in 1689, was the grant of an aid of six monthly assessments on real and personal property, exclusive of stock on land, which was declared exempt. Two further aids were granted during the same year on the same terms as the first. These three aids amounted, in the year 1689-90, to a tax of 4s. in the pound on the yearly rental of real property, and 24s. for every £100 of personal property (except debts, stock on land, and household goods); or 4s. in the pound on £6, the then legal interest of money, thus rating both descriptions of property alike. They produced the sum of £2,018,704. This mode of assessing the land tax was adopted with some slight variation until the year 1697, when another important change was introduced, by which the State was deprived of its right to a growing revenue from the increasing value of property.

It was provided, by the various Acts passed during the early years of the reign of William and Mary, that the tax on land should be paid on the " full true yearly value thereof at the time of assessing thereof." Upon this principle the tax was voted annually until 1697, when the arrangement made with the nation in in 1689 was deliberately set aside. By the land tax Act passed in 1697 a fixed sum of £1,484,015 was granted which was to be paid first by personal estate (except desperate debts, stock on land, household goods, and loans to his Majesty) and employments of profit, except military and naval. Then lands, tenements, &c., were to be " charged with as much equality and indifferency as was possible by a pound rate, for or towards the said several and respective sums of money by this Act set and imposed." The effect of this statute was first to levy a fixed rate on personal property and offices of emolument, and then to make up any deficiency in the amount voted, by a rate on real property. Nothing is said in the act about any valuation of real property, and, in consequence of this omission, the last valuation made prior to the passing of that act has been the one employed from that time to the present. In the following year (1698) the same sum was voted, and from that date, the sum to be raised by the land tax was voted yearly in the same way until the year 1798, when it was made perpetual at the amount then levied.

It is obvious that the designation of this tax, as imposed in 1697, was inaccurate, and that it would have been more correctly described as a property tax.

It soon became, however, really, as well as nominally, a land tax, the assessment of personal property being abandoned, although it was not relieved by statute until the year 1833. The exemption of personalty seems to have been effected gradually, and it does not appear that, at any period, the officers of the revenue have been able to assign any reason for this evasion of the law. It is obvious, however, that as personal property increased in value, the assessment of the land tax at a fixed rate upon that description of property, as provided in the statute, would have produced more than was necessary to meet the sum voted by parliament. In that case land, which it was provided was to be taxed merely to supply the deficiency of personalty, would have entirely escaped. A writer on the subject, previously quoted, expresses his conviction that the act upon which all subsequent land tax acts were based was skilfully framed so as to throw the chief burden of the tax on personalty, which was subsequently gradually relieved from assessment, in order to prevent that enquiry into the mode in which parliament had dealt with the tax, which its enforcement upon personalty according to the letter of the law, would necessarily have provoked. One fact is certain, that during the whole of the period in which personalty was liable to the tax from 1697 to 1833, the landed interest was supreme in the House of Commons, and the result of that supremacy is seen in the successive measures they adopted to relieve themselves from burdens upon their property, which were the legitimate and advantageous commutation of the heavier obligations of the feudal system.* The mode in which this branch of the public revenue has been appropriated, since the abolition of feudal tenures in 1660, by a powerful section of the community was fitly described by Mr. Cobden, in 1842,† as an example of legislative fraud scarcely surpassed by the Corn Laws."

It has been seen already that in 1798 the tax was made permanent by Mr. Pitt, and the amount to be contributed by each parish fixed by statute. This was done with a view to the early redemption of the tax, in order to provide funds for the War. The measure, however, was not successful, the amount redeemed being much less than was anticipated. In fact the tax had become so insignificant in its amount that the yearly payment was a smaller burden than the trouble of redemption. The amount redeemed can be easily ascertained; in 1798 the produce of the tax was £1,989,673; in the year ending 31st March, 1869, it was £1,131,301, showing that the amount redeemed during fifty years was £858,372. Of this sum £435,888 was redeemed in the years 1798-99.‖ The maintenance of the valuation of 1695 for the land tax produces some remarkably grotesque

---

* The above remarks have been mainly summarised from the Pamphlet previously referred to—" The Constitutional Right to a revision of the Land Tax "—which contains full details of the mode in which this Tax has been treated, with copious references to the original documents. See also Sinclair's History of the Revenue, and McCulloch's Treatise on Taxation.

† Corn Law Debate, March 14, 1842.

First Inland Revenue Report, 1857, pp. 38-39, and App. pp. 30-32.

results. In some parishes the tax amounts at the present time to 10 per cent. of the rental, in others to 5 per cent., while in some instances it is but a halfpenny or a farthing in the pound, and in the case of Liverpool it is less than the thirty-sixth part of a penny in the pound.* In fact it has ceased to be a tax, and has become simply a small rent charge created on certain lands in favour of the State.

If the land tax had been invariably assessed according to the evident intention of the Act, 12 Car. 2, cap. 24, upon the actual rent, a very considerable revenue would now have been derived from that source. If the four shillings in the pound was a fair assessment in 1660 it would not have pressed unjustly upon the increased assessments, which the augmented value of the soil would have created. In his lectures on Political Economy, Professor F. W. Newman argues that a tax of even 50 per cent. upon rent, if imposed at the period when it first became generally payable, would have been a perfectly unexceptionable source of revenue.† In parting with the ownership of the soil it was quite competent for the State to have imposed a rent charge of one-fifth upon the landlords, the remaining four-fifths of the rental being retained by them as their remuneration for the management of the estates. It is difficult to estimate with accuracy what would have been the full effect of such an arrangement upon the amount of their rentals. There is

---

* Returns of Land Tax Valuation, Parliamentary Paper, Session 1844, No. 316.
† Lectures on Political Economy, 1851, p. 211.

little doubt that the heavy burdens so long imposed upon trade and industry by duties of customs and excise have exercised a powerful influence in retarding the development of national prosperity, and have materially diminished the amount that, under more favourable conditions, would have accrued to the landed proprietors. The transfer of their legitimate obligations to the people by the substitution of excise duties, for the obligations previously imposed upon them, was not by any means a profitable bargain. The remission of burdens upon land, which had existed for centuries, at the expense of the consumers of commodities was neither more nor less than a fraud upon the community, unattended by any corresponding advantage to the class, in whose supposed interest it was perpetrated.

CHAPTER XVII.

PROPERTY AND INCOME TAX.

An attempt to levy an Income Tax was first made by Mr. Pitt in 1798, in the form of an addition to the assessed taxes, regulated by the amount of income possessed by the persons who were subject to the payment of the duties then imposed. It was intended as an aid and contribution for the prosecution of the war, but in that respect it disappointed the expectations of its projector, the amount it yielded during the year being only £1,855,996. In consequence of this failure, the duties imposed in 1798 were repealed in the following year, and, in lieu thereof, a tax of 10 per cent. was imposed on all incomes of £200 and upwards. Incomes below £60 were exempt from taxation, and incomes between that amount and £200 were charged at reduced rates. The new tax produced the sum of £6,046,624 during the first year of its existence; and being found a profitable source of revenue, was continued until the year 1802, when it was repealed in consequence of the peace of Amiens. It was re-imposed on the renewal of the war in the following year, and, subject to modifications in detail, formed an important constituent in the fiscal system of Great Britain until the peace of 1815, when it was again repealed. The net receipt of this tax during the ten years ending 1816 was £129,041,299, a yearly average of above £12,900,000.* The causes which led to its revival by Sir Robert Peel, in 1842, must be well known to all who are acquainted with the history of that period. A fresh generation has, however, come into existence since that year, and it may, therefore, be necessary briefly to recount the facts of the case. For several years the revenue had suffered from a chronic deficiency, which was estimated, by Sir Robert Peel, for the year 1842-3, at £2,570,000; and for the six years ending 1843, unless remedial measures were applied, at £10,072,000. Every interest in the kingdom was in a condition of intense depression; it was stated in the House of Commons that half the mills in Lancashire were closed, and that the fixed capital of that county had depreciated within a few years fully 50 per cent.; a similar condition of affairs prevailed in other manufacturing districts; shipping was an unremunerative property; agricultural distress had been for a lengthened period the constant topic of discussion in Parliament, and enquiry by Select Committees; the number of able-bodied paupers had increased more than two-fold since 1836; the number of

---

* First Inland Revenue Report, 1857, pp. 30-31. App., p. cxxvii.

emigrants had risen from 44,478 in 1835 to 128,344 in 1842, and would have been far larger if the people had possessed the means with which to defray their passage; in the district of Manchester 8,000 persons were living on 15d. each per week, and in that and other manufacturing districts thousands of workpeople were wandering through the streets in search of employment. The industry of the country had been " protected " with such success, that the exports of British produce and manufactures were not equal in value to those of the year 1815, and the home demand was materially diminished through the absence of remunerative employment. It was to provide a remedy for this deplorable condition of affairs that Sir Robert Peel proposed the re-enactment of the Income Tax. It is a noteworthy fact that, in this instance, as well as in 1798, an attempt had been made to provide for the deficiency of revenue in another way. In 1840 the Whig Government proposed, with the approval of Sir Robert Peel, and carried successfully through Parliament, an increase of 10 per cent. on all the assessed taxes except the post horse duty, and 5 per cent. on all duties of Customs and Excise, except those on spirits which were increased 4d. per gallon, and corn, in which no alteration was made. The anticipated gain to the revenue from these sources was £2,186,000, the actual increase only £677,485. In the following year the Ministry were defeated on a vote of want of confidence and dissolved Parliament, the question submitted to the constituencies being the acceptance or rejection of a fixed duty on corn. In the new House of Commons the Ministry found themselves in a minority of 91, and Sir Robert Peel took office at the head of a Conservative and Protectionist administration, with the avowed intention of maintaining the existing Corn Laws. The first task imposed upon him was that of providing for the chronic deficiency of the revenue, and in 1842 he proposed the re-enactment of the Income Tax appealing to owners of property to make a temporary sacrifice, for the purpose not only of supplying the deficiency, but of enabling him with confidence to propose great commercial reforms, which would afford a hope of reviving commerce, and such an improvement in the manufacturing interest as would react upon every other interest in the community.* Intended as a temporary expedient the Income Tax has remained a permanent feature of our fiscal system; it has been renewed upon several occasions for the purpose of securing further remissions of indirect taxation; it has been increased to provide for the expenses of several wars, and to defray the large additions to our naval and military expenditure which followed the Crimean War. The various changes in the rate of the tax, and other modifications introduced since 1842, are shown in the following table :†—

---

* For more complete details respecting the renewal of the Income Tax, see Fiscal Legislation, 1842-65. Longmans. pp. 8-17

† Parliamentary Paper, Sess. 1862, No. 316. Twelfth Inland Revenue Report, App. p vii. Acts of Parliament, 31 Vic. c. 28 32 and 33, Vic. c. 14.

Year in which the change was made.	Rate in the £ on £150 and upwards. s. d.	Rate in the £ on £100 to £150. s. d.
1842-3*	7	nil.
1853-4	7	5
1854-5	1 2	10
1855-6	1 4	11¼
1857-8	7	5
1858-9	5	5
1859-60	9	6½
1860-1	10	7
1861-2	9	6

£100 and upwards.

An abatement allowed of the duty on £60 from Incomes under £200.

1863-4	7d.
1864-5	6
1865-6	4
1867-8	5
1868-9	6
1869-70	5

Farmers assessed on half their rent in England, and one-third in Scotland and Ireland.

The Income Tax has been described, with great accuracy, by Mr. Dudley Baxter,† as "not so much a tax as a code of taxes, bringing within its jurisdiction income of every description, from land, from houses, from farming, from the funds, from trades and professions, and from public salaries and pensions." The following table shows the various schedules under which it is assessed, the amount of

---

* In Great Britain only, extended to Ireland in 1853.

† Taxation of the United Kingdom, p 26.

income, and the produce of the tax for the year ending 31st March, 1869:*

Schedule	Description	Rate in the £ d.	Amount Assessed. £	Amount Collected. £ s. d.
A	Lands, tenements, and hereditaments	6	132,273,709	
B	Occupation of lands			
	England	3	30,453,918	
	Scotland, Ireland	2¼	7,053,751	
	Nurseries and market gardens	6	84,698	
	Compositions for tithes and tithes leased...	1⅞	2,085	8,743,462 10 0
C	Annuities, dividends, &c.	6	33,689,568	
D	Professions, trades employments, mines, ironworks, railways, and similar undertakings	6	160,978,671	
E	Salaries and pensions paid out of public revenue...	6	22,005,866	
	Total		£386,542,366	

In the enactment of the Income Tax in 1842, Sir Robert Peel followed the example of Mr. Pitt, and confined its operation to Great Britain. The exemption of Ireland from the tax was discontinued in 1853, on the plea that she had received her full proportion of the benefit attending previous remissions of taxation, obtained through the income tax which Great Britain had hitherto borne alone, and would also profit largely by the remission of taxation

* Parliamentary Paper, Sess. 1869, No. 427.

then proposed; at the same time the balance of the debt due from Ireland to England on account of advances for the establishment of the Poor Law in Ireland and the Irish Famine, amounting to £4,500,000, was remitted.*

In the same year the tax was extended from incomes of £150, the limit fixed by Sir Robert Peel, to incomes of £100, which were assessed at a lower rate of duty. This arrangement was continued until the year 1863, when a uniform rate was adopted for all incomes, commencing at £100 a year, but an abatement of £60 allowed on incomes under £200. In consequence of this arrangement the owner of an income of £100 pays the tax on £40 only, the owner of £200, on £140; and intermediate incomes in like proportion.

A very important mitigation of the tax was introduced in 1853, by the exemption of sums invested in deferred annuities or policies of insurance, to the extent of one-seventh of the whole income. This measure was a concession to the principle, advocated by Mr. Mill and other economists, that savings ought to be exempt from taxation. It is true that it only meets the requirements of one form of saving; the question naturally arises if such investments are exempt, on what principle are other savings held liable to the tax? The only answer to this question is the one given by Mr. Gladstone, upon the introduction of

---

* Mr. Gladstone's Financial Statements, pp. 58-60, 71-73.

the exemption just named, that he did not think it possible to make provisions of that kind applicable to savings simply as such. There are, no doubt, difficulties in the way of a universal application of the principle, but it surely cannot be an utter impossibility to produce *bonâ fide* evidence of all monies invested as savings, whatever may be the form such investments may take.

These are the main features of the tax, and are common to all its schedules. The pressure of the tax varies according to the nature of the income assessed, and it has therefore been found convenient to make each schedule the subject of a separate chapter.

Before proceeding to the consideration of the various schedules in detail, there is one objection very commonly urged against this tax, which deserves notice—the assessment of permanent and precarious incomes at the same rate. In defence of this practice, it is argued that the State protects the income of the year, and that, therefore, the tax should be assessed upon the income of the year exclusively, irrespective of the source from which it may be derived. There is a simplicity about this argument which is rather captivating, especially to the owners of permanent incomes. It will, however, hardly bear investigation. In protecting real property the State protects not merely present, but also future income; the owner may die within the year, but his property remains, and along with it the income it produces. In the case of professional and trading incomes, which depend upon the continuance of physical and mental powers, the income itself terminates with the ability of the individual to pursue his avocation. In the one case the State protects permanent property, in the other precarious earnings; it can hardly be alleged that services so dissimilar are of equal value; if they are not, with what show of justice can the present mode of equal assessment be maintained? It is, unquestionably, the fact that the general opinion of the community is most decidedly opposed to this feature of the Income Tax, and it is difficult to believe that it can long be maintained upon a footing, so entirely repugnant to the prevailing sentiment of those by whom it is paid.

The Committee of the House of Commons, appointed in 1852 to inquire into the then existing mode of assessing and collecting the Income Tax, examined many witnesses upon this point. Among them was Mr. Mill, who advocated the exemption of all savings from taxation, but, if that plan should prove impracticable, he would adopt that of taxing temporary or precarious incomes at a lower scale than permanent incomes. If real or permanent property be taxed at 7d. in the £ on the net income, he would tax temporary incomes at 7d. on three-fourths of the net income, and those that are not only temporary, but precarious, at 6d. in the £ on three-fourths of the net annual income. The capitalization of incomes and levying the tax upon the value so ascertained was advocated by the following actuaries: Mr. S. Brown, Mr. C. Jellicoe, Mr. Peter Hardy, and Mr. G. P. Neison; by Dr. William Farr, the Registrar-General, and by Mr. J. R. Jeffery, of Liverpool. Other modes of rendering the tax more equitable were suggested by Mr. Erskine Scott and Mr. T. R. Edmonds, actuaries. Mr. Babbage and Mr. Henry Warburton supported the uniform assessment of income from whatever source derived. The committee made no report, on the ground that the state of business and the prospect of an early prorogation did not afford sufficient time for discussing and preparing one that would do justice to the subject. The evidence presented to Parliament contains a mass of valuable information on this important subject.*

---

* First and Second Reports of Select Committee on the Property and Income Tax. Sess. 1852, Nos. 354, 510. For summary of the evidence referred to, see Mr. Hume's Draft Report, pp. xxviii., xxix. of Second Report.

CHAPTER XVIII.

INCOME TAX, SCHEDULE A.—LANDS, HOUSES, ETC.

This schedule of the Income Tax is now the only contribution to the public revenue assessed upon the rental of real property, and paid out of the net income of the landlords. It has been already shown that the land was formerly the principal source of the revenues of the Crown, that the Land Tax imposed originally at 4s. in the £ on the clear annual value of the land has dwindled away, under the influence of landowning Parliaments into a small rent charge levied upon a portion only of the lands of the kingdom. In 1798 the amount to be contributed by each parish to the Land Tax was fixed in perpetuity with privilege of redemption if desired, and in the following year a tax on incomes was introduced, which, in the case of owners of real property, was a tax upon rent. From that period to the termination of the war real property was assessed, by the Property and Income Tax, in a mode analogous to that intended by the original Land Tax of William and Mary. In the year 1815, however, by the repeal of the Income Tax, the owners of real property were relieved from any direct payments on account thereof; the heavy burdens laid upon trade and industry during the war by means of duties on home productions and foreign imports were retained, but land, formerly the chief source of revenue, became but only tangible property exempt from taxation. The impolicy of this proceeding is now almost universally acknowledged ; its results were seen in depression of trade, diminution of the demand for labour, increase of pauperism, and deficiency of revenue, until at length the re-imposition of a direct tax became an imperative necessity.

The amount of income assessed under this schedule of the Income Tax during the last three financial years was as follows :—*

Year ending 31st March,	£
1867	154,119,601
1868	125,070,065
1869	132,273,709

Increase of 1869 over 1868, £7,203,644.

The decrease of property assessed in 1868 and 1869 compared with the year 1867, arises from the transfer of the profits of several commercial undertakings, previously assessed under this schedule, to schedule D, to which they more properly belong. The tax upon such undertakings will, therefore, be considered under the schedule in which they are now placed.

Judging from the mode in which the land tax was dealt with by Parliament, the objections raised by the landed proprietors to the income tax, and the readiness with which they repealed it in 1815, and have reduced it whenever practicable, a tax on rent would appear to

---

* Parliamentary Paper, Taxes and Imposts, Session 1867, No. 545 ; Session 1868, No. 463 ; Session 1869, No. 427.

be very unpopular with the owners of land. It is an ostensible burden, but is infinitely less onerous and prejudicial to owners of real property than duties of Customs and Excise, which are none the less deleterious because their operations are concealed from sight. There can be no doubt that the "temporary sacrifice" which Sir Robert Peel demanded from holders of property in 1842 has proved a permanent advantage. By means of the Income Tax duties have been removed, not merely from the prime necessaries of existence, but from nearly every article of luxury consumed by the rich; simultaneously with this process, the liberated industry of the community has steadily increased the value of real property.

A tax on the rent of land was denounced by Mr. McCulloch, in his work on Taxation, as extremely objectionable, on the ground that it had always been, and would unavoidably continue to be, a formidable barrier to agricultural improvements. In his opinion it was far preferable to levy duties on the luxuries consumed by the proprietors of land.* Since the publication of these speculations, a policy the exact reverse of the one he recommended has been pursued by successive administrations. Taxes upon luxuries have been, one by one, repealed, through the instrumentality of a direct tax falling upon rent in common with other kinds of income, until there is no luxury, mainly consumed by the wealthy, subject to taxation but

---

* McCulloch's Treatise on Taxation, 1845, pp. 43-56.

wine. It does not appear, however, that agricultural improvement has been checked, or that landed proprietors have suffered any diminution in their rents. On the contrary, the value of land has materially increased, and improvements have been introduced into the practice of agriculture, much greater in extent and importance than at any previous period of our history.

A complete test of the accuracy of the opinions, enunciated by Mr. McCulloch, is to be found in the income tax returns of different periods. Let us, therefore, enquire to what extent his views have been verified by facts. During the period commencing with the year 1815, when the tax was repealed, and terminating with the year 1842, when it was re-imposed, there was no imperial tax levied upon the rent of land, while the luxuries of the rich were subject to numerous duties. The gross rental of land in England and Wales for the year 1814-15, according to Parliamentary returns, was £34,330,462, or allowing 10 per cent. for the depreciation of the currency, £30,897,416. In the year 1842-3, it was £40,167,089, showing a total increase, in 28 years, of £9,269,673, or an annual average of £331,059.*

In 1842 the Income Tax was revived for the purpose of enabling Sir Robert Peel to propose remissions of taxation upon trade and industry. In 1845 further relaxations, mainly of taxes upon necessaries of life,

---

* M'Culloch's British Empire, ed. 1847., vol. 1, pp. 553-4.

took place; in 1846 the principle of free trade in corn was adopted by Parliament; and in subsequent years numerous other duties of customs and excise have been repealed or reduced. The benefits of the free trade policy were not, however, immediately experienced so far as agriculture was concerned. It was a misfortune that the Conservative party did not accept free trade as an accomplished fact in 1846, but maintained an unwise and delusive agitation for the restoration of protection, which was not terminated until the decisive verdict of the general election of 1852. As a natural consequence of such a policy the energies of the farmer were mainly directed to political agitation, not to the introduction of such agricultural improvements as were rendered necessary by his altered circumstances. According to the evidence of Mr. Jas. Caird,* in 1852, the most antiquated and wasteful practices were then to be found side by side with the few modern improvements then introduced, but little progress having in many cases been made for nearly a century. In numerous instances he witnessed the same rude processes which were recorded by Arthur Young, eighty years previously; scientific cultivation was then the exception, the "wisdom of our ancestors" the rule, in agricultural pursuits. It is not, therefore, to be wondered at that during the period of purely political agitation, which immediately followed the repeal of the Corn Laws, there was but little increase

---

* Caird's English Agriculture, 1852, pp. 498-500.

in the rental of the kingdom. The amount assessed in England and Wales under schedule A for rent of land in the year 1852-3 was £41,086,269,* an increase over 1842-3 of £919,180, the yearly average being only £91,918. The year 1852-3 may be fairly taken as the concluding year of the protectionist era. It was then that the farmers finally abandoned all idea of the re-enactment of the Corn Laws, and set to work to meet their altered circumstances. If the rental of that year is compared with that of the year 1815 it will be seen that the increase during 37 years was £10,188,853, the annual average of the period being £275,374.

It is now our task to enquire into the effect of the free trade policy which was inaugurated, and indeed, rendered practicable, by the levy of direct taxation on income, including rent. It does not appear, from the returns since 1852, that the landowners have suffered in consequence of the change. The increased value of land in England and Wales is shown in the following table.

Year.	Value of Lands Assessed under Schedule A. £	Increase £
1852-3	41,086,269	
1856-7†	41,176,957	over 1852-3 90,688
1864-5‡	46,403,437	over 1856-7 5,226,480

* Property and Income Tax Return, Sess. 1860, No. 592.
† Ibid.
‡ Tenth Inland Revenue Report, 1866, App. p. lx.

The annual average increase for the 8 years ending 1864-5 being £653,310.

The following are the returns for Scotland during the same periods:*

Year.	Value of Lands Assessed under Schedule A. £	£
1814-15	5,075,242	
1842-3	5,586,527	Increase over 1814-15 511,285
1852-3	5,499,404	Decrease compared with 1842-3 87,123
1856-7	5,932,156	Increase over 1852-3 432,752
1864-5	6,830,639	898,483

It appears, from these figures, that the increased rental of land in Scotland for the year 1864 compared with the year 1852, was £1,331,235, or 24 per cent.; while, in England and Wales, the increase during the same period was £5,317,168, or about 12¾ per cent. An enquiry into the conditions under which the practice of agriculture exists in England, as compared with Scotland, will no doubt demonstrate that the growth of rent in the latter portion of the island has been stimulated because superior security is afforded to capital invested in agriculture. A very competent authority says,† in reference to the system of yearly

---

* First Inland Revenue Report, 1857. App. p. cxxix. Property and Income Tax Returns, Sess. 1845, No. 102, and Sess. 1860, No. 592. Tenth Inland Revenue Report, 1866, p. ix.

† On the Conditions of Agricultural Success. By George Hope, Fenton Barns. Transactions of the National Association for the Promotion of Social Science 1863: Longmans, p. 778.

tenancy, so largely prevalent in England, " I feel perfectly amazed that public policy should permit such a state of matters to continue. In Scotland no such difficulty is felt, and even on the most strictly entailed estates, leases for 19 and 21 years are universal. There is not a doubt that this fact has had much to do in placing Scotch Agriculture in the high position it at present holds, and that it has enabled Scotch farmers to pay rents higher in amount than is obtained for naturally richer soils in the more genial climate of the South."

It must be evident from the statistics already quoted that a tax on rent is not necessarily a hindrance to the improvement of agriculture. Uncertainty of tenure, the consequent insecurity of capital employed in the cultivation of land, which is its invariable attendant, and fiscal restrictions upon trade, manufactures, and employment are the real evils against which the landowners have had to contend. In throwing the weight of taxation upon commodities consumed by the population, and thus relieving their estates from the direct tax, which was imposed in lieu of feudal tenures, the landholders of England conferred no real benefits upon their descendants. In proportion as trade and industry have been liberated from fiscal exactions, and mainly indeed in consequence of such liberation, the people have become more prosperous, and improvements in agriculture have been rendered imperative in order to meet the increased demand for agricultural produce, which is the natural result of the growing prosperity of the community. The distressed condition of the agricultural interest, which during the era of protection was the standing topic of Parliamentary discussion, has long ceased to occupy that position, and the landowners, according to their own admission, have no reason whatever to regret the increased freedom of commerce, which was rendered possible by direct taxation.

The following table shows the increase in the value of house property assessed since 1815.*

	England and Wales. £	Scotland. £
1814-15	14,895,130	1,364,270
1842-43	35,556,399	2,919,338
1852-53	40,621,408	3,847,004
1859-60	48,779,076	4,988,840
1864-65	59,285,537	5,801,551

It appears from these figures that the increased rental of houses or messuages in England and Wales for the year 1842-3, over the year 1814-15, was £20,661,269, an annual average for the twenty-eight years of £737,902. The increase of the year 1864-5 over 1842-3 was £23,729,138, an annual average during twenty-two years of £1,078,597. In Scotland the increase of the two periods was respectively £1,555,068 and £2,882,213, the annual average being respectively £55,538 and £135,555. The large reductions of expenditure which resulted from the termination of the French War stimulated the growth of

---

* First Inland Revenue Report, 1857. App. p. cxxix. Property and Income Tax Returns, Sess. 1845, No. 102, and Sess. 1860, No. 592. Tenth Inland Revenue Report, 1866, p. lx.

manufactures, and consequently added largely to the rental derived from houses, shops, factories, and other buildings used for trading purposes. In the last year of the war (1814) the amount expended for naval and military purposes,* including the interest of the debt, was £101,738,072, a large part of which was sent abroad in the shape of subsidies to foreign Governments, and consequently was abstracted from the capital of the nation. During the twenty-two years ending 1814, no less a sum than £46,289,459 was expended upon our allies in direct money subsidies, in addition to supplies of clothing and other stores, the value of which it is impossible to ascertain. The expenditure for the year 1816 was upon a much smaller scale than that of 1815, being only £65,169,771; in the following year it was reduced to £55,281,238, the average for the twelve years ending January 5, 1828, being £55,909,000. About that time a strong demand arose for further retrenchment, which resulted, in the year 1829, in a reduction of about £5,600,000, the annual average of the twelve years ending January 5, 1840, being £48,220,000.†

A review of the finances of the United Kingdom since 1842 presents a remarkable contrast, as far as expenditure is concerned. The repeal of numerous taxes has been attended by a steady increase in the amount of taxation, which appears to have grown in

---

* Progress of the Nation, 1847, p. 514-518.
† Ibid, p. 483.

an almost equal ratio with the ability of the people to bear the burden. The increased assessment of Schedule A, since that year, has not been produced in any degree by a diminution in the gross amount of taxation, but solely by a more judicious accommodation of the burden, by means of which the productive power of capital and labour has been augmented, and the country been made prosperous, in spite of the large increase in the public expenditure. It may be urged in opposition to this view that we are now experiencing stagnation in trade and a considerable diminution of employment, which shows an unhealthy and dangerous condition of affairs. This is no doubt true, and if it continue as long as similar periods of commercial depression during the protective era, it will no doubt ultimately affect rent and depreciate the value of real property. If the course adopted on previous occasions of commercial vicissitude be examined, it will be found that the true remedy for the existing distress is to be sought in a further remission of indirect taxation. The encouragement of imports is the readiest way of increasing our exports; rents advance with advancing commerce. A progressive condition of trade is the most desirable one for landlords. If they would increase the value of their property, they will act wisely in urging upon Parliament a further development of the principle of free trade, although it may involve an increase in the amount of their direct contributions to the national revenue. An additional tax on property, in order to secure the immediate repeal of a large portion of the remaining duties of customs and excise, with a view to the gradual extinction of all restraints upon freedom of exchange, would prove a wise investment on the part of owners of real property.

The Income Tax was not extended to Ireland until the year 1853, and the various items comprising Schedule A, as far as that portion of the United Kingdom is concerned, were not distinguished until the year 1861-2, so that a detailed comparison cannot be made even for the short period that the Irish landowners have contributed to this tax. The following are the assessments for the years 1861-2 and 1864-5 :*—

	1861—2. £		1864—5. £
Lands	8,990,830	...	8,893,060
Messuages	3,333,783	...	3,670,106
Manors	59	...	812
Fines	32,214	...	27,037

In comparing the assessments of England, Scotland, and Ireland, it must not be forgotten that in the two former instances, lands and houses are assessed upon the full annual value or rack rent, while in Ireland they are assessed on the Poor Law Valuation, which the Inland Revenue Commissioners believe to be at least 20 per cent. under the true value, making the total rental about £15,000,000, instead of £12,500,000.

The burdens placed on land have been a long

---

* Tenth Inland Revenue Report, 1866. App. p. lx.

standing ground of complaint, which may be appropriately noticed in the present chapter. It does not appear that the landholders have any special ground of complaint at the present time, the proportion of the burden borne by them having been considerably reduced. In a paper read at the last annual meeting of the British Association, by Mr. Purdy, it was shown that, while sixteen years ago landed property, including the tithe rent charge, bore 45·6 per cent. of the aggregate local and imperial burdens, in 1864—5 it bore only 35·3 per cent. This relief has been obtained by the great increase in other descriptions of property, in the creation of which the Income Tax has been a powerful instrument, having made the repeal of more obnoxious and wasteful taxes a possibility. It cannot be denied that, as far as strictly Imperial taxation is concerned, real property has for a very long period been highly favoured, if indeed a policy which hinders the full development of its value can justly be considered a favour. The main ground of complaint relates to the incidence of local burdens, which it is alleged increase the price of food. These taxes, however, fall mainly upon rent, which is not an element in the price of agricultural produce. Under a system of Free Trade prices are regulated by competition; rent being the surplus of profit after the cultivators of the soil have been remunerated for their capital, skill, and industry. If local burdens could by any possibility be abolished, the permanent gainers would be the landlords; that portion of the surplus profit, which is now paid in the shape of local rates, would find its way into their pockets.

There is also another aspect of the question, very frequently overlooked. In so far as taxes upon property are of long standing they partake of the nature of rent charges, and are not any burden whatever upon the present holders, who have purchased or inherited their estates subject to these responsibilities. The diminished percentage of the public burdens now borne by the land, compared with the burden of sixteen years since, shows that, as a class, the landowners have not any valid grievance. If local rates increase, the pressure falls, in the first instance, upon the tenant, but if the increase becomes permanent it ultimately forms a deduction from the rent, which the landlord would otherwise have received. A considerable portion moreover of local taxation, such as highway and drainage rates, is necessary to render the estates upon which such improvements are effected productive to their owners, and cannot be regarded as special burdens in any other sense than investments in machinery are special burdens upon millowners and manufacturers. As respects the Poor Rates there can be little doubt that the Poor Law system, as administered in the rural districts, is one cause of the low rate of wages which prevails. If there were no poor law, and the agricultural labourers were compelled in consequence to make that provision against old age, which is common among other classes, there would of necessity be an increase in the rate of wages. This increase would be met, not by trenching upon the profits of the agriculturists, which are regulated by the facilities for the employment of capital in other pursuits, but by a deduction from the rentals of the landowners. A thorough investigation into the incidence of local taxation, especially that of the rural as compared with town districts, would not disclose any serious cause of complaint on the part of the landed or farming interests. It must also be borne in mind, in considering this question, that landowners have secured from the government peculiar facilities of borrowing money from the State at low rates of interest, and on easy terms of repayment. This is a great advantage which they enjoy over other sections of the community; though it is fairly open to question whether such an interference on the part of the government with the legitimate operations of private enterprise has been altogether advantageous to the community at large.

CHAPTER XIX.

INCOME TAX, SCHEDULE B.—OCCUPATION OF LAND.

The profits of farmers are assessed, for income tax purposes, upon the amount of one-half their rental in England and Wales, and one-third in Scotland and Ireland. Mr. McCulloch describes this as the very best plan that could be devised for assessing such incomes,* though it is difficult to see on what ground it can be defended, except that farmers are such imperfect or negligent accountants that they would be quite unable to render any statement of their profits, like those which are required from other traders.

In the year 1851 a new provision was introduced, intended to meet the objection that farmers who had not made the assumed profits were compelled by the law as it stood to pay the full amount of their assessment. By the Act 14 Vic. c. 12, permission was given to persons gaining their livelihood principally by husbandry, in the event of their not having realised

---

* Treatise on Taxation, 1845, p. 131.

the assumed profit, to attend before the District Commissioners and obtain relief by the reduction of the charge to the amount of profit they had actually made. The number of applications made under this provision has been very small, and it may, therefore, be fairly assumed either that there is no real grievance in this mode of assessment, or that persons engaged in husbandry are not able to present accounts for the consideration of the commissioners which show a diminution of profits below their estimated rate.

The following table shows the net rental assessed at different periods since the imposition of the tax in 1842.*

	England and Wales. £	Scotland. £
1842-3†	21,202,216	2,435,040
1853-4†	24,835,288	2,905,080
1857-8	26,842,243	3,397,365
1864-5	29,153,450	3,918,451

These figures show the amount paid as rent by farmers liable to the tax, and therefore indicate the extent to which the landlords of purely agricultural lands have been benefited since the year 1842. The returns are no doubt modified by two circumstances, the extension of the tax in 1853 to incomes between £100 and £150, and the consolidation of small holdings. In the latter case, however, it may be fairly assumed that consoli-

---

* Income Tax Return, Sess. 1860, No. 136. Tenth Inland Revenue Report, 1866. App. p. lix.

† The figures in this return give the net profits assessed, which are in England one half, and in Scotland one third the actual rent.

dation takes place with a view to increased rent. After every possible allowance has been made for the influence of these two circumstances it cannot be denied that the return presents a very satisfactory aspect as regards the landed proprietors. It is also certain that these increased rents would not accrue, unless the farmers themselves were securing an adequate remuneration in return for the employment of their capital and skill in the pursuit of agriculture.

The net amount assessed in Ireland in 1855-6 was £2,574,684, and in 1864-5 £2,946,072,* the assumed profit being one-third the amount of the rent. This assessment, like that of schedule A, being made upon the Poor Law Valuation in Ireland, and not on the full value as in Great Britain, the actual rental in 1864-5 would appear to be about £3,500,000.

---

* Tenth Inland Revenue Report, 1866. App. p. lix.

CHAPTER XX.

INCOME TAX, SCHEDULE C.—DIVIDENDS FROM PUBLIC REVENUE.

This schedule includes all incomes derived from dividends in the Public Funds and in Foreign Government Securities. In the imposition of the Income Tax upon the fundholders, Sir Robert Peel followed the example of Mr. Pitt, and treated these dividends in the same way as any other kind of income, notwithstanding the provision that they should be paid "free of all taxes and charges whatsoever." It is difficult to understand in what respect such a proceeding differs from simple repudiation of a portion of the public debt unless, indeed, some equivalent were bestowed upon the fundholder. It was justified by Sir Robert Peel on two grounds: first, that other taxes were repealed which pressed more heavily upon consumers, so that a reduction was made in the cost of living to a greater extent than the amount of tax imposed; secondly, that the tendency of his financial policy was to improve the value of the funds, which rose to the extent of 4 per cent. within a few weeks of the introduction of the budget of 1842. The former of these reasons, it is evident, does not apply to foreigners holding investments in the funds, and it was upon the argument that no distinction was made in any Act of Parliament between native and foreign fundholders, and that the rise in value, which followed the proposal of his budget in 1842, enabled any foreigner, who wished to escape the tax, to sell out on very favourable terms, that he justified the imposition of the tax upon such dividends. There can be no doubt that liability to taxation affects the market value of these securities, and that in consequence of this fact the original injusitce has been remedied, present holders having purchased or inherited subject to taxation.

The amount of income assessed under this Schedule for the year 1842-3 was £27,909,793; for the year 1864-5 it was £30,889,559; and in Ireland, not subject to the tax in 1842, £1,154,930.* The annual interest of the funded debt of the United Kingdom having been decreased to the extent of two millions sterling since 1842-3, by the falling in of the long annuities, the increase in this Schedule arises from investments in Foreign, Indian, and Colonial securities. Objection has been taken by some writers on taxation to the imposition of taxes upon income derived from foreign investments, which it is urged should be taxed only in the country from which such income is derived The argument against such taxes is based upon the principle, that the subjects of every State ought to

---

* Property and Income Tax Return, Sess. 1852, No. 399. Tenth Inland Revenue Report, 1866, App. p. 57.

contribute in proportion to the revenue, which they respectively enjoy under the protection of the State, and that such income is protected by the State in which it accrues, not by that in which it is expended. If the country in which such income is expended is fairly entitled to tax it, and the country from which it is received follow our example in respect to foreign holders in our funds, it is evident that it may be taxed twice over. The only valid defence of a tax upon incomes derived from foreign investments appears to be that of Sir Robert Peel, that a tax upon income is less burdensome than taxes upon commodities, from which no description of income can escape; and that, in consequence of the substitution of the one for the other, holders of foreign securities derive a benefit greater than the burden imposed upon their dividends.

The amount assessed under this Schedule in England is £32,500,000, and in Ireland £1,115,000, but this does not represent the amount contributed by each country, as all the investments of Scotland, Ireland, the Colonies, and Foreigners in our own public funds, and in foreign securities, are placed to the account of England, in which country the dividends are made payable.*

---

* Twelfth Inland Revenue Report, 1869, p. 25.

CHAPTER XXI.

INCOME TAX, SCHEDULE D.—PROFITS OF TRADES, PROFESSIONS, AND EMPLOYMENTS.

The amount of income assessed under this Schedule was largely increased in the year 1866, by the transfer from Schedule A of the profits of quarries, mines, ironworks, and similar undertakings, in compliance with the 8th Section of the Act 29 Vic. c. 36. This transfer is one of those changes which introduce an element of confusion into the returns of the tax. In order to make a more accurate comparison of the growth of profits at different periods, it is desirable to confine our our attention in the first instance to such descriptions of income as have been always assessed under this Schedule, comprising the profits of ordinary trades, professions, and employments, incomes from property not assessed in other Schedules, and profits earned abroad by residents in the United Kingdom.

It is difficult to arrive at any accurate estimate of the rate at which profits of trades and professions have increased at different periods since 1814, owing to the want of returns showing exactly corresponding items. The amount of profits, assessed under Schedule D, in 1814 was £37,058,987, of which £13,604,639 consisted of incomes below £150; the amount assessed on incomes of £150 and upwards being £23,454,348.* In the year 1842-3, when the tax commenced at £150, the amount assessed was £57,663,496,† shewing a total increase in such incomes, compared with the years 1814-15, of £34,209,148, the annual rate being £1,221,755. From this, however, some allowance must be made for that portion of the amount assessed, which consisted of incomes from trade below £150, belonging to persons having other property, which, added to their income under this Schedule, rendered them liable to the tax. The analysis of the returns of the year 1864-5, published by the Inland Revenue Commissioners, does not give the details of incomes between £100 and £150. It is, therefore, impossible to institute an accurate comparison between that year and the year 1842-3. If it is assumed that one-half of the incomes between £100 and £200 are below £150, it would seem that the total amount assessed at £150 and upwards in 1864-5 was £95,480,636,‡ the increase over 1842-3 being £37,817,140, and the annual rate £1,718,960. On the supposition that these figures are correct, it will be seen that the yearly increase in profits, commencing with incomes of £150, during the twenty-two years ending 1864-5, has been nearly £500,000 in excess of that of the twenty-eight

---

* First Inland Revenue Report, 1857, App. pp. 130-31.

† Income Tax Return, Sess. 1860, No. 136.

‡ Tenth Inland Revenue Report, 1866, App. pp. lxii-lxiii.

years ending 1842-3. It is a fact worthy of notice in connection with this increase in the rate of profits that the growth of population in Great Britain was considerably less during the latter than it was during the former period. The exemption of Ireland from the tax until the year 1853, renders it impossible to make any comparison of the income of that portion of the United Kingdom for similar periods.

The following table gives the amount assessed in each of the three Kingdoms for the ten years ending 5th April, 1867.*

Year ending 5th April	England & Wales £	Scotland £	Ireland £	Total £
1856	67,832,390	6,718,656	4,336,674	78,887,720
1857	69,110,522	6,856,106	4,280,182	80,246,810
1858	73,106,832	7,107,287	4,510,470	84,724,589
1859	73,444,998	6,779,421	4,587,457	84,811,876
1860	76,990,577	7,382,513	4,627,922	89,001,012
1861	77,824,790	7,176,475	4,604,257	89,605,522
1862	81,120,368	7,893,125	4,677,568	93,691,061
1863	85,088,087	8,234,777	4,673,743	97,996,607
1864	87,307.979	8,536,243	4,368,610	100,212,832
1865	95,636,761	9,799,026	4,669,979	110,105,766
1866	103,908,302	10,942,857	5,296,536	120,147,695
1867	135,504,680	15,644,661	7,054,716	158,204,057

During the whole of the above period the tax commenced with incomes of £100. The returns for 1867 are largely augmented by the transfer from Schedule A of railways, mines, ironworks, gasworks, &c. It

---

* Tenth Inland Revenue Report, 1866, App. p. lxiii. Twelfth, ditto, 1869, App. p. xiii.

might, perhaps, be considered reasonable that full and precise information should be given by the Inland Revenue Commissioners of the effect of this change; this, however, has not been done. It appears that the increase in the profits of trades and professions, for the year 1866-7 over 1865-6, including railways, mines, ironworks, and gasworks, in England and Scotland, was £7,549,000, so that £30,507,362 of the total increase of Schedule D may be assumed to be mainly due to the transfer of railways, mines, ironworks, &c.* The total assessment of Schedule A for 1866-7 was £125,249,705, of which £1,963,000 was the increased assessment of "houses" over 1865-6. This amount deducted from the return for 1866-7 reduces the gross assessment of 1865-6 on lands, houses, manors, and fines to £123,286,705. The total assessment of Schedule A for that year being £154,119,601, it would seem according to the figures of this Schedule that £30,832,896 was the amount transferred from the one schedule to the other, an excess of £325,534 as compared with the preceding estimate, which it would have been easy for the Commissioners to explain. The difference is no doubt composed of the increased assessments of mines, ironworks, and gasworks in Ireland, and of quarries, fisheries, canals, and other undertakings in the United Kingdom.

The increase on trades and professions for the year 1866-7 was £4,019,000 in England, £1,099,000 in

---

* Twelfth Inland Revenue Report, 1869, pp. 17-19. App. p. xiii.

Scotland, and £630,000 in Ireland, these amounts added to the figures of the previous year make the assessment for the year 1866-7 as follows:—

	£
England	107,927,302
Scotland	12,041,857
Ireland	5,927,536
Total	125,896,695

It will be seen that the rate of increase in incomes derived from trades and professions compared with that of the two preceding years shows a considerable diminution, the returns of the years 1864-5 being £9,892,934 in excess of those of 1863-4, and those of the year 1865-6 being £10,041,929 in excess of the year 1864-5, while the increase of the year 1866-7 over the year 1865-6 was only £5,749,000. This is no doubt attributable to the panic of 1866 which swept away so many banks and joint stock companies. It is, however, a noteworthy fact that the only district which showed any considerable decrease was the City of London, where the greater number of such companies had their head quarters. The falling off in that district amounted to £1,052,000; the assessment for 1865-6 being £24,653,000, and for 1866-7 £23,601,000.* The investments of persons resident in all parts of the United Kingdom and elsewhere in public companies, whose head offices are in London, are assessed there, thus swelling the English return.

---

* Twelfth Inland Revenue Report, 1869, pp. 18-19.

The investments of the Irish themselves, say the Commissioners, in Irish Companies are assessed to Income Tax not unfrequently in London, where the head offices of the companies are situated.

There can be no doubt that the substitution in 1842 of a tax upon the profits of trades, professions, and employments in lieu of the duties of Customs and Excise, then reduced or repealed, has been productive of great advantage to the trading and manufacturing community. A tax on income causes much less interference with production and exchange, than duties of Customs and Excise. It leaves industry free, it imposes no restraint upon trade, it presents no obstruction to the creation of wealth, and in its economic results it is in every respect superior to any form of indirect taxation. It has proved a powerful resource in war, and a beneficent instrument of industrial and commercial advancement in peace. Notwithstanding these advantages it has been invariably regarded with dislike by a large section of the mercantile and trading community, by whom every reduction of the tax has been hailed with satisfaction. At the termination of the Crimean War it was the war income tax which aroused their hostility; the war duties on tea and sugar were not reduced for many years. The opposition of the trading class in 1842, before they had experienced any of the benefits which this tax was destined to secure for them, may be easily understood; but that a commercial people should prefer the reduction of a tax on profits to the removal of restrictions upon trade, after they had experienced the beneficial results of such a course of legislation, is somewhat marvellous. If the original rate of 7d. in the pound had been maintained as the minimum, it is clear that many imposts which place restraints upon the development of the trade of the country might long since have been entirely repealed. The two main objections urged against the tax are, first, its inquisitorial nature, especially that portion of its machinery which involves the disclosure of private affairs to Commissioners, who may be neighbours and possibly rivals in trade; and, secondly, the injustice of taxing incomes from trades and professions, (which, inasmuch as they depend upon the continued health of those who earn them, are precarious,) at the same rate as incomes derived from realised property. These are evils capable of remedy; and it would have been far more conducive to their real interests if the trading community had directed their energies towards securing a more perfect form of direct taxation instead of systematically urging upon Parliament the reduction of the Income Tax.

A far more serious evil in connection with this impost is the wholesale manner in which it has been evaded by means of false returns. In 1853 Mr. Gladstone referred, in his budget speech, in illustration of this evil, to claims made by twenty-eight persons in the City for compensation for loss of business during the construction of Cannon-street. They claimed £48,159 as one year's profits, and obtained from the jury £26,973, the amount at which they had returned themselves to the Income Tax Commissioners being only £9,000.* In the annual reports of the Inland Revenue Commissioners, frequent instances in which such evasions of the tax have been discovered are regularly recorded. In their latest report,† the Commissioners say, " the claims to compensation which have arisen out of a recent extensive demolition of houses in a certain district by the Metropolitan Board of Works have given the usual evidence of the frauds which prevail in returns under Schedule D." It appears that in this case 200 claims for compensation were examined by the Inland Revenue officers, in 80 of which surcharges were made and sustained upon appeal. The aggregate of taxable incomes returned by the parties themselves was £73,642, the amount ultimately found correct was £171,370, being in excess of the returns by £97,728, or about 130 per cent. The Commissioners then proceed to estimate the probable loss from this source, taking, for the purposes of their calculation, the year 1864-5. After remarking that the practice is not confined to any particular class, trade, or profession, but has been found prevailing in the case of legal practitioners claiming compensation on the abolition of exclusive privileges, on all occasions of demolitions of property for great public works, and in the accounts of great public companies and firms having world-wide reputations, they state their opinion that the sum on which

---

* Financial Statements, 1863, pp. 28-29.

† Twelfth Inland Revenue Report, 1869, pp. 19-24.

duty was evaded, in the year 1864-5 was £57,254,997. At the then rate of 6d. in the pound, this would have added £1,431,374 to the revenue, or about the produce of a penny on the whole tax. If accuracy is to be expected in any case it might, perhaps, be assumed in that of public companies. The report, however, dispels this delusion by the publication of eleven instances in which the total amount returned was £308,573, the amount ultimately assessed being £577,214; in a twelfth instance no return was made, and the assessment was ultimately fixed at £63,949. In these twelve cases the amount unreturned was £332,590. From another report* we learn that one joint stock company, which returned £6,000 as assessable profits, ultimately paid on £88,000, and that another, which returned £190,000, was finally compelled to admit that the true return should have been £250,000.

The opinion of the Commissioners as to extensive evasions of the tax receives considerable confirmation from the return of persons assessed under schedule D, at various amounts, in the United Kingdom,† which will be found on the next page. A similar fact is noticed by the Special Commissioner of the Revenue of the United States in his report for the year 1869, in respect to the assessment of the Income Tax in that country.

---

* Tenth Inland Revenue Report, 1866, p. 42.
† Ibid. App. pp. lxii lxiii.

Assessment to Schedule D for 1865-6.	Number Assessed.	Amount of Profits. £
£100* Under	72,290	3,155,059
£100 and under £200	167,535	14,776,975
200 ,, ,, 300	46,773	10,306,036
300 ,, ,, 400	20,316	6,492,813
400 ,, ,, 500	10,501	4,385,440
500 ,, ,, 600	7,828	4,016,413
600 ,, ,, 700	4,555	2,810,574
700 ,, ,, 800	2,891	2,088,690
800 ,, ,, 900	2,493	2,031,368
900 ,, ,, 1,000	1,136	1,041,620
1,000 ,, ,, 2,000	7,716	9,835,270
2,000 ,, ,, 3,000	2,307	5,309,026
3,000 ,, ,, 4,000	1,188	3,904,098
4,000 ,, ,, 5,000	655	2,805,341
5,000 ,, ,, 10,000	1,327	8,855,282
10,000 ,, 50,000	891	16,939,995
50,000 and upwards	110	11,351,766
Total	350,512	£110,105,766

It seems incredible that, in the whole of the United Kingdom, there are only 655 persons, engaged in trades and professions assessed at incomes between £4,000 and £5,000. The following instances of deficient returns are given in one of the reports previously referred to :—†

Returns £	Assessment £
1,800	6,000
2,000	9,000
750	4,900
1,000	4,000
1,000	2,344
1,000	2,376

---

* Having income also from other sources.

| Twelfth Inland Revenue Report, 1869, pp. 20-22

The excuses offered in cases of detection, in order to obtain a mitigation of penalties, disclose a belief in the mind of the parties proceeded against that this mode of returning their incomes is by no means singular. In one case a person returned his income in 1865 at £250; he was surcharged and assessed at £400. In the year 1867, a Metropolitan Improvement being imminent which would include his premises, he returned his profits at £1,000 and was surcharged at £1,900, which on appeal was confirmed by the District Commissioners. His excuse was that he did not know what his income really was; it will be observed, however, that as soon as he began to anticipate that his premises would be required by the Metropolitan Board of Works, he voluntarily increased his assessment from £400 to £1,000. In another case a return of £1,200 in 1865 was increased to £1,500 in 1866, and £2,000 in 1867. A surcharge was made in order to compel the parties to produce their accounts, when it was found that they were liable to assessment in 1867 on £3,311. In justification of themselves they urged that " their returns bore fully as large a proportion to their actual income as the returns made by their competitors and others in trade;" and that to have made true returns " would have been in effect to penalise themselves." In another case no return was made for four years, during three of which, 1864—5—6 the firm was assessed at £800 and in 1867 at £1,000. The accountants employed in making their claim for compensation fixed the average profits for the four years at £1,477.* It is useless to multiply instances, which if necessary might easily be done. Sufficient evidence has been adduced to show that the practice of making false returns prevails to a very large extent. In many instances the errors are no doubt unintentional, but inasmuch as the tax on lands and houses, on dividends, and on salaries and pensions of public officers is levied nearly to the uttermost farthing which is due, it is evident that, as far as the principle of taxing all incomes equally (irrespective of the source from which they are derived) is concerned, the income tax is practically a failure.

In the financial statement of 1853, Mr. Gladstone in alluding to such evasions of Income Tax made the declaration that "the exemption of one man means the extra taxation of another." That this is the case there can be no doubt; but it would be somewhat difficult to show in what material respect evasion of taxation, by means of a false return, differs from evasion of taxation by abstaining from taxed commodities. The result so far as other taxpayers are concerned is identical, and yet a portion of our fiscal system has been praised by its advocates because it is voluntary; no man need pay it unless he likes. It matters little to A with an income of £1,000 a year whether B with a like income throws an undue burden upon him by making a false return, or by abstaining from taxed commodities and thus escaping indirect taxes to which

---

* Twelfth Inland Revenue Report, 1869, p. 20.

A contributes. In both cases the same result is produced, the exemption of B involves the extra taxation of A. In this respect duties of Customs and Excise stand upon the same ground as Schedule D of the Income Tax. The real difference consists in the fact that in the one case the State is a party to unequal taxation by making the payment of taxes depend upon the taste, whim, caprice, or necessities of the taxpayer; while in the other the same result is produced by fraud or negligence in making the return required by the law.

Inequality of taxation is, however, a small evil compared with the demoralising effects which are inevitably produced by the habit of making false returns. If the practice spread and become general, as the disclosures previously referred to unquestionably indicate that it has, a most deleterious influence must be exerted upon the morals of the trading community. It was one of the strongest arguments employed against high duties of Customs and Excise, that they promoted crime by rendering the practice of smuggling profitable. It can hardly be alleged that a system of direct taxation which opens the door to such frauds as have been from time to time disclosed in respect to the Income Tax, will produce no evil results. The transition from a fraud upon the Government to a fraud upon the public is comparatively easy, and there is much reason to fear that commercial morality has not been advanced by the laxity with which merchants and traders have assessed themselves to the Income Tax.

The profits transferred in 1866, from Schedule A include "Quarries, Mines, Iron-works, Gas-works, Salt Springs or Works, Alum Mines or Works, Waterworks, Streams of Water, Canals, Inland Navigations, Docks, Drains and Levels, Fishings, Rights of Market, and Fairs, Tolls, Railways and other ways, Bridges, Ferries and other concerns of the like nature, from, or arising out of, any Lands, Hereditaments, or Heritages."* It is impossible to form an accurate comparison of the profits of each separate class of undertaking for the years 1814—15, 1842—43, and 1864—65, owing to the imperfect nature of the earlier returns. In the year 1814—15, Quarries, Mines and Ironworks are the only works mentioned separately, the remainder being included under the head of "general profits," which also contained profits arising from Lands, Tenements, Hereditaments, or Heritages not in the actual possession or occupation of the party to be charged. The last amount assessed under the head in 1814—15 was £65,257. The following table shows the amount assessed on Quarries, Mines and Ironworks in Great Britain at three different periods.†

	1814—15 £	1842—43 £	1864—65 £
Quarries	70,378	240,483	582,217
Mines	678,787	2,081,387	4,743,406
Ironworks	637,686	559,435	1,798,431
	1,386,851	2,881,305	7,124,054

* Act 29 Vict., c. 36.

† First Inland Revenue Report, 1857. App. p. cxxix. Real Property Return, Sess. 1845, No. 102. Tenth Inland Revenue Report, 1866. App. pp. lx., lxi.

It will be seen that the increase of these three heads, in 1842—43 over 1814—15, was 107 per cent., while in 1864—65 over 1842—43 it was 147 per cent. The most noteworthy fact in connection with this table is the decreased income from Ironworks in 1842—43 as compared with 1814—15. It does not appear that protection had proved an advantage to that branch of British Industry. The returns of our Export Trade corroborate this view, the Exports of British Manufacture entered under the head of Iron and Steel being as follows :*—

			£
1815	...	...	1,280,962
1842	...	...	2,457,717
1868	...	...	15,036,398

If we take Hardwares and Cutlery the contrast is even more striking, a considerable decrease having taken place between 1815 and 1842; the values were as follows :—

			£
1815	...	...	2,349,662
1842	...	...	1,398,487
1868	...	...	3,854,742

The following table gives the remaining items of this schedule for the years 1842—43 and 1864—65.†

---

* The Earl of Liverpool on Foreign Trade, 1820. Hatchard & Son App. p. 54. Statistical Abstract, 1842—1856, p. 20. Annual Statement, 1868, p. 31.

† Real Property Return, Sess. 1845, No. 102. Tenth Inland Revenue Report, 1866. App. pp. lx—lxi. The figures for 1865—6 are those of Great Britain only, Ireland not being subject to the tax in 1842.

	1842—43 £	1864—65 £	Increase.
Fisheries	58,914	96,003	61¾ per cent.
Railways	2,598,942	15,654,723	502 per cent.
Gasworks	not entered separately.	1,763,787	205 per cent.
Other Property.	1,509,884	2,842,791	
			Decrease.
Canals	1,307,093	870,112	33 per cent.
			Increase.
Add Quarries, Mines, and Ironworks	2,881,305	7,124,054	147 per cent.
Total	8,356,138	28,351,470	239 per cent.

The return for 1842-3 includes, under the head of other property, some income not derived from the undertakings transferred to Schedule D. The sum of £1,509,884 has, therefore, been estimated on the supposition that the relative proportions of income assessed as "other property" and "general profits" were the same in 1842-3 as in 1864-5. It is probable, therefore, that the above figures are not strictly accurate, but the substantial result will not be materially affected. It will be seen that railways form a very important feature of this section of the Income Tax Assessment, but on every other description of property, except canals, which have no doubt suffered from the formidable competition of railways, there is also a satisfactory increase.

The following table shows the respective amounts assessed in England, Scotland, and Ireland, and the totals for the United Kingdom in 1864-5. *

---

* Tenth Inland Revenue Report, 1866. App., pp. lx-lxi.

	England. £	Scotland. £	Ireland. £	United Kingdom. £
Quarries	526,049	56,168	8,005	590,222
Mines	4,276,567	466,839	85,983	4,829,389
Iron Works...	1,247,597	550,834	—	1,798,431
Fisheries	30,913	65,090	12,004	108,007
Canals	785,809	84,303	29,605	899,717
Railways	13,882,200	1,772,523	920,853	16,575,576
Gas Works ...	1,618,071	145,716	84,735	1,848,522
Other property	2,485,831	356,960	60,762	2,903,553
Total	£24,853,037	£3,498,433	£1,201,947	£29,553,417

The items comprised under the head of "other property" are salt springs or works, alum mines or works, docks, drains and levels, rights of markets and fairs, tolls, bridges and ferries.

CHAPTER XXII.

INCOME TAX. SCHEDULE E. PUBLIC OFFICES AND PENSIONS.

This Schedule includes every public office or employment of profit, and every annuity, pension, or stipend payable by Her Majesty, or out of the public revenue of the United Kingdom, except annuities and dividends from the public funds, which are assessed under Schedule C. The amount of income assessed under this head at different periods has been as follows:*—

	Great Britain. £	Ireland. £	Total. £
1814-15	14,823,783	not	
1842-43	9,718,454	liable.	
1855-56	16,082,655	925,767	17,008,422
1864-65	19,293,924	1,157,242	20,451,166

It appears, at first sight, from the above figures, that there has been, since 1842, an increase of 98 per cent. in the amount paid in salaries and pensions. This result, however, is considerably modified by the

---

* Property and Income Tax Return, Sess. 1852, No. 399. Tenth Inland Revenue Report, 1866, App. p. lviii.

extension of the Income tax in 1853 to incomes of £100 a-year. In that year the increased produce of this Schedule was 12 per cent., nearly the whole of which may be fairly attributed to the extension of the tax. The same fact will also modify the figures of the following years, as compared with 1842-43. The returns for 1855-56 and 1864-5 show an increase of 20 per cent. for the whole United Kingdom in nine years. It may, therefore, be fairly supposed that the increase of 1864-5 over 1842-3 is fully 75 or 80 per cent. There can be no doubt that this Schedule is collected very fully, the amount of Government salaries, pensions, and superannuations being accurately known. It is equally certain that evasions of the tax by the mercantile community throw a heavier burden upon officials with fixed salaries than they would otherwise have to bear, whether they are in the service of the Government or of private firms. In either case they have no means of evading payment of the tax, their incomes being in the one instance known to the heads of their departments, and in the other returned by their employers.

The same remarks apply to this as to other schedules, in reference to the assessments of Great Britain and of Ireland. The officers of public companies are charged at their head offices, and nearly the whole of the civil servants of the Crown. Even the public servants employed in Ireland and abroad, are for the most part charged in England.

CHAPTER XXIII.

MODE OF PAYMENT OF TAXES.

"The people must pay, and not know it; must be deceived a little, or they would not pay after this fashion." In this extract from a sermon by the late Theodore Parker,[*] there is a very pithy summary of the main argument employed in favour of the mode of paying taxes, by means of which two-thirds of our revenue are collected. Taxes paid, not as direct contributions to the State, but in the price of commodities, are obtained surreptitiously; the people pay and do not know it; they imagine they are purchasing tea, coffee, sugar, beer, spirits, or tobacco, when in every instance a large portion, in some an excessively preponderating portion, of the price they pay, is for the tax imposed upon the article they purchase. The arguments generally used in favour of this system of collecting the revenue were very forcibly refuted by Dr. Channing in the following words:[†]—"we attach

---

[*] Collected Works of Theodore Parker. Trübner & Co. 1863. Vol. IV., p. 12.

[†] Dr. Channing's Works. Griffin & Co. 1840. The Union—p. 119.

no importance to what is deemed the chief benefit of tariffs, that they save the necessity of direct taxation, and draw from the people a large revenue without their knowledge. In the first place, we say, that a free people ought to know what they pay for freedom, and to pay it joyfully, and that they should as truly scorn to be cheated into the support of their Government, as into the support of their children. In the next place, a large revenue is no blessing. An overflowing treasury will always be corrupting to the governors and the governed. A revenue rigorously proportioned to the wants of a people, is as much as can be trusted safely to men in power."

Taxes are usually divided into two classes, direct and indirect; the former are paid, as their name implies, directly, to a servant of the Government; the latter, indirectly, to dealers in taxed commodities, by whom the tax is advanced, and then recovered, with a profit thereon, in the price of the articles sold. It has been held by some writers on taxation that, inasmuch as some direct taxes are analogous in their economic effects to indirect taxes, the above distinction is inaccurate, and that the term indirect should include all taxes which tend to restrict consumption, whether they are levied directly or indirectly. There have been numerous controversies upon this question, but it is better, upon the whole, to adhere, as far as possible, to the actual meaning of the words employed as definitions; neither is it advisable to conceal the fact that direct taxation may be applied in a form which is economically unsound. The grand distinction between the two systems is, that while direct taxation may, indirect taxation must be pernicious in its effects upon trade and employment, and unjust in its incidence upon the taxpayer.

"Every tax ought to be levied at the time, or in the manner in which it is most likely to be convenient for the contributor to pay it."* This is the principle laid down by Adam Smith, and adopted by subsequent economists in relation to the collection of the Revenue. This is not, however, the sole condition; one of still greater importance being economy in the cost of collection. In the words of Adam Smith:—"Every tax ought to be so contrived as both to take out and to keep out of the pockets of the people, as little as possible, over and above what it brings into the public treasury of the State." A tax may comply perfectly with the first condition, and at the same time offend flagrantly against the second. For example, taxes upon commodities may be said to be paid at times most convenient to the taxpayer; he pays them "little by little, as he has occasion to buy the goods." This advantage will be found, however, to be more than neutralised by the increased cost to the taxpayer involved in this mode of collecting a revenue. It must be obvious that any inconvenience to taxpayers, arising from the periodical payment of taxes, may be met by voluntary appropriations of weekly or monthly proportions of income, and in this way all

---

* Wealth of Nations. Book V., Chap. II., Part 2.

the advantages of taxes upon commodities may be secured without any of their drawbacks. All prudent persons make arrangements for the payment of their rent, and might, with equal ease, do so for the payment of their taxes.

By the Customs and Inland Revenue Duties Act, 1869, the provisions made by previous Acts for the payment of the land tax, the duties on inhabited houses, and the income tax (excepting such as are payable by way of deduction, or are assessable in respect of railways) were repealed. In lieu thereof these taxes are made payable on or before the 1st day of January in each year, not in advance, as many people have supposed, but for the year commencing on the 25th of March previous to, and terminating upon, the 5th of April following. By this arrangement the taxes which would otherwise have been payable in July and October, are not due until January, the sole payment in advance being for the quarter ending the 5th of April. This has been the mode of payment previously in force in Scotland, without causing any objection on the part of the taxpayers of that country. In fact, it is difficult to understand what reasonable ground of complaint can exist in respect to an arrangement which allows the taxpayer to retain capital in his own hands which would otherwise have been paid to the Government in the shape of taxes, at least three months previously to the period when they are now demanded.

By the same Act (32 and 33 Vic., c. 14) the duties of assessed taxes levied in Great Britain were repealed from the 6th of April, 1869, in England, and the 25th of May, 1869, in Scotland, and in lieu thereof license duties on servants, carriages, horses, and armorial bearings were substituted. These licenses are placed under the control of the Excise, and are payable before the end of the month of January in each year. The regulations under which they are issued have already been described. The complaint urged against the new arrangement is that it makes a whole year's land, house, income, and assessed taxes payable in the month of January when other heavy payments are usually demanded. The observations previously made in reference to the convenient time of payment assumed in the case of taxes on commodities, are applicable to the mode of collection now under consideration; no inconvenience has been felt in Scotland from this arrangement; in fact, it merely requires the exercise of prudence to enable the taxpayer to provide for this annual payment. There are some facts which those who grumble at the new arrangement overlook. First, they have credit for at least six months' land tax, income tax, and House Duty; secondly, no assessed taxes were demanded for ten months of the year 1869, the taxes payable during the year ending 31st March, 1870, being for servants employed and articles used during the year ending 31st March, 1869; thirdly, the arrangement of which they complain enabled the Chancellor of the Exchequer to propose the repeal of the following taxes :—*

---

* Parliamentary Return. Taxes and Imposts. Session 1869. No. 427

	Amount produced in 1868-9.
	£
Corn, meal, flour, and 14 similar articles	915,585
Fire Insurance	1,070,046
Tea License	72,778
One Penny of the Income Tax	1,457,243
	£3,515,652

In addition, the following trade licenses were repealed from the 1st of January, 1870 :—

	£
License to let post horses	142,196
Hackney carriage licenses and duties	106,159
Stage carriage licenses and duties	42,798
	291,153

The assessed taxes were also reduced and simplified. The Fire Insurance Duty was repealed from midsummer, and the Tea License from July 5, 1869. The entire remission was estimated by Mr. Lowe as follows :—

	£
Taxes repealed	2,520,000
Modification of the assessed taxes	420,000
	£2,910,000

In considering the effect of the changes, introduced by the Budget of 1869, in the collection of taxes, it is not just to overlook the remissions of taxation, of which it was the instrument. Would the present objectors have preferred the continuance of a sixpenny Income Tax, of the Fire Insurance Duty, and of the other taxes then repealed? If not, it is difficult to see in what respect they have any valid reason for the outcry they have made.

The remainder of the direct taxes, including trade licenses (except such as are levied according to the quantity manufactured), legacy and succession duties, stamps, and law-fees are payable at various times, generally upon the receipt or payment of money, and appear, on the whole, to be collected without any serious inconvenience. Those who admire the convenience of collecting a revenue by means of Customs and Excise Duties are apt to overlook the fact, that the facility of easy payment may be dearly purchased. If the effect of such duties is invariably to limit trade and thus diminish the means of purchasing, it must be obvious that the convenience of such taxes is apparent only, not real. It is of no advantage to establish convenient modes of payment if the ability to pay is thereby diminished.

CHAPTER XXIV.

COST OF COLLECTION OF TAXES.

A far more important consideration, than the mode of payment, is the cost of collection. Direct taxes as a rule cost the taxpayer nothing beyond the amount he actually pays to the tax collector. There are, no doubt, exceptions to this rule, but not to any considerable extent. Mr. Dudley Baxter points out, in his work on Taxation, that the income tax on Schedule A being assessed on rack-rent with no allowance for repairs, insurance, cost of management, or abatements of rent, becomes on a tax of 5d. in the pound, $2\frac{1}{3}$ per cent. on the net income an increase of one-third per cent.; that the Land Tax costs the landowners £2,037,000 instead of £1,093,000, the sum of £944,000 having been redeemed; that the probate duty being paid out of capital is a tax of $2\frac{3}{3}$ per cent. on the income derived from such property, and that the legacy duty on personal property, and property devised for sale becomes a tax of $3\frac{1}{3}$ per cent. on income, instead of the $2\frac{1}{2}$ per cent. which is received by the State.* As respects the income tax assessed to Schedule A in Ireland his remarks do not apply, the tax being levied on the Poor Law valuation, which is 20 per cent. below the actual value. The assessment of land and houses in Great Britain for the year 1866-7, according to the Inland Revenue report,† was £112,358,424; if we allow 16 per cent. deduction, the net rental will be £94,406,277 upon which an increase of one-third per cent. amounts to £314,687. With respect to the redemption of the Land Tax, the excess to which Mr. Baxter alludes is not paid by the owners of lands still subject to the tax, and it may be presumed that the redemption was a profitable bargain for those who voluntarily commuted their annual payments for a fixed sum. There is no doubt that the payment of Probate and Legacy duty, if valued upon the income derived from legacies, increases the per centage of the tax; these imposts are, however, taxes upon property, not upon income, they are ostensibly paid out of capital inherited, and do not exact from the receiver of a legacy more than the actual per centage at which the tax is levied. The £12,659,760 paid for Land and Income Taxes, and for the Probate and Legacy Duty in 1868-9 was the full amount paid by the taxpayer. This is also the case with other direct taxes, but when we come to investigate the cost of indirect taxation we arrive at a very different result.

---

* Taxation of the United Kingdom, pp. 130-132.

† Twelfth Inland Revenue Report, 1869. App. p. xiii.

The cost of collecting the Customs Revenue has been discussed by the Commissioners of Customs on several occasions. In two of their Annual Reports they claim to have the following items of expenditure excluded from the cost of collection :—*

	£
Expense of the Statistical Department	52,644
Expenses under Merchant Shipping Act	19,500
Collection of Light Dues	2,400
Miscellaneous functions of an extraneous character ...	7,820
Rent, law charges, &c., connected with Do.	5,000
Overtime and special attendance	10,250
	£77,813

The Commissioners also claim, in both reports, to deduct the expenses of the warehousing department on the ground that it is not in any way accessory to the collection of the revenue, but simply a postponement of the just dues of the Crown for the advantage of the merchant. The present Commissioners may perhaps be excused the inaccuracy of this statement, as their experience may not comprehend the period prior to the introduction of the warehousing system, and they are not presumed to study very closely the history of even their own department. Against their opinion, that of the late Mr. G. R. Porter may very fairly be placed. He considered that among the practical advantages that attended the adoption of the warehousing system were the simplification of the Custom-house accounts, the abridgement of labour in

---

* Fourth Customs Report, 1860, pp. 21—24. Seventh Report, 1863, pp. 22—23.

the revenue departments, and the prevention of systematic and extensive frauds by which large fortunes had been created.* It appears therefore that it has some connection with the collection of the revenue. Independently of these considerations it is quite a sufficient answer to the allegations of the Commissioners to say that customs duties being emphatically taxes upon consumption, should be levied, not upon importation, but as nearly as possible at the period of actual purchase by the consumer. It is also deserving of their consideration whether, in these days of increasing commerce, the continuance of the Custom House would be possible, unless its evils were mitigated by some arrangement of the kind. If there were not duties there would be no warehousing system. The Commissioners also claim to deduct the expenses of the Coast Guard, now under the control of the Admiralty, on the ground that it performs other functions. In so far as it is employed in the protection of the revenue, this service is an item in the cost of collection. The expense during the last year in which it was exclusively under the control of the Custom House, 1855, was £450,000. It is also alleged that superannuations and compensations ought not to be included, but these payments are as certainly incurred in connection with the revenue as the salaries of officers who are actively employed therein. The whole question of such payments is one well deserving of consideration. It would probably be conducive to

---

* Progress of the Nation, 1847, pp. 473—474.

efficiency, if servants of the Crown were placed upon the same footing as servants of the Mercantile Community: so long, however, as these payments are made, they are clearly items in the cost of collection.

The amount paid for the expenditure of the Customs Department for the year 1868-9, according to the Finance Accounts,* was £915,737, to which should be added £5,804 advanced out of revenue, beyond the amount due from the Treasury at the commencement of the year,

Making a total of	£951,541
The Coast Guard Service expenditure estimated at ..	450,000
Increases the actual cost to	1,401,541
From this deduct extraneous expenses, adding £3,000 for examining Foreign Cattle; and taking the expenses under the Merchant Shipping Act at £6,000, the sum voted by Parliament, the remainder being provided by the Board of Trade	66,953
The balance	£1,334,588

will show the actual cost of collecting the revenue of the Customs. The net produce of the duties collected in the United Kingdom was £22,291,645; in the Isle of Man† £12,532; the Spirit duties collected for the Inland Revenue £1,522,385; other receipts, except Fees under Merchant Shipping Acts and Payments from Merchants for special Services, accounted for in

---

* Finance Accounts, 1868-9.

† The Expenses of the Inland Establishments were first included in the Estimates for 1868-9.

the amount deducted from cost of collection, £93,342; making the total net revenue collected by the department £23,919,904, at a cost of £1,334,588, or 5½ per cent. This result differs no doubt from that arrived at by the Commissioners of Customs, on the principle laid down in their seventh annual report, of excluding the Coast Guard and Superannuations. The cost of collecting £24,099,617, in the year 1868, was, according to their method of calculation, only £3 5s. 10d. per cent. The omission of such important items of expense as have been mentioned would not be considered satisfactory in any mercantile balance sheet, and there is no reason whatever for placing the Customs establishment on a different basis.

The amount paid for salaries and other expenses in the Inland Revenue department, for the year 1868—9, was £1,591,950. The revenue collected, deducting £1,522,385, spirit duties collected by the Customs, was £41,309,320, showing a cost of £3 17s. per cent. The expenses of collection of each separate branch cannot be ascertained. In the case of both Customs and Excise, the interest and capital expended in the purchase and erection of Custom Houses and other revenue offices, the repairs and renewal of furniture, and some other expenses, ought to be added in order to arrive at the exact cost, upon sound commercial principles. Detailed information upon these points is, however, inaccessible, and we must therefore be content to ascertain the annual charge for Salaries and Superannuations.

The cost of collection to the government does not, however, represent the actual cost to the taxpayer. In the case of duties of Customs and Excise the profits of traders converted into tax-gatherers must be added. The amount of revenue so collected (including those Brewers' and Malsters' Licenses, which increase with the quantities produced,) is, in round numbers, £40,380,000. Upon the capital employed in the payment of these taxes, the traders, by whom they are advanced, charge a profit as certainly as they do upon that portion of their capital which is invested in the articles themselves. The problem for solution is:— how much does this process add to the cost of collection?

A writer in the "Produce Markets Review,"* after describing minutely the hindrances, delays, and expenses, in which Merchants are involved by the system of import duties, says:—"All this trouble, expense, serene officialism, delay and inconvenience, have, of course, eventually to be paid for by the public, in addition to the duty. The goods generally have to go through another middle-man's hands before reaching the shopkeeper. In this case buyer number two's profit is calculated on the original cost of the article, plus the duty, plus the merchant's expenses in dealing with the Customs, and plus buyer number one's expenses in paying the duty, his profit upon it, and

---

* December 5th, 1868.

on the merchant's expenses, and all these items have to be added to the original cost by the retail buyer who next gets the goods, before he adds his charge for selling to the public. Thus, it is estimated, with fair probability of accuracy, that a net revenue, for instance on Tea, of say in round numbers £2,300,000, actually costs the public in England not £2,300,000 but nearly £3,900,000, or a clear loss of £1,600,000; or again, a revenue which could be raised directly by 2d. in the pound on the income-tax, costs really, raised indirectly, a sum equal to 3d. in the pound."

The case of sugar, as described in the same article, is even stronger, the effect of graduated duties being an encouragement of slovenly production and waste, to such a degree that "Sugar which, with Free Trade, ought to cost the public £10 a ton, plus 8 per cent., or less than £11, actually costs them £31 per ton, or three times what it ought to cost. In other words, without duties, Sugar would in a few years be sold in England at 1½d. per lb., while it now costs 4½d. Put in another way, the £5,550,000 revenue returned by Sugar, in round numbers, really costs £13,000,000, as it raises the cost of the 600,000 tons of Sugar we use yearly, from a cost, at £11 per ton, of £6,600,000, to a cost, at £32 per ton, of £19,000,000; or, to obtain indirectly what would be 4d. in the pound on the income tax, we tax our possible incomes 1s. in the pound."

The collection of the Malt Tax is equally costly,

if the calculations of its opponents are correct. Mr. E. S. Cayley, the well-known anti-Malt Tax Advocate, estimates that it it costs £10,000,000 to collect the £6,000,000 of revenue derived from this article.* It was stated by Sir Fitzroy Kelly, in the House of Commons, that the £60,000,000 spent upon beer would be reduced to £40,000,000 if the Malt Tax were repealed.† Mr. Joshua Fielden of Todmorden (now M.P. for the West Riding), in his evidence before the Malt Tax Committee, 1868, entered into calculations showing that the successive profits of the malster, brewer, and retailer, increased the tax from 21s. 8d. per quarter to 31s. 6d., or 45 per cent.‡

If we examine the more moderate estimates of Mr. Dudley Baxter as to the effect of such taxes upon price, we obtain the following result :§—

Articles.	Duty. £	Per Cent.	Additional Cost of Duties. Amount. £
Tea, Coffee, Chicory, and Cocoa	3,100,797	10	310,079
Wine, Beer, and Spirits	23,918,069	31	7,414,598
Tobacco	6,542,461	15	981,369
	£33,561,327		£8,706,046

The estimate for tea is low; in making it a probable

---

* Malt Tax Report 1867, p. 82-85.
† Malt Tax Debate, April 17, 1866.
‡ Malt Tax Report 1868, p. 145.
§ The Taxation of the United Kingdom, pp. 132-140.

rise in price consequent upon the abolition of the duty has been taken into account, 10 per cent. being the full benefit which Mr. Baxter believes the consumer would derive from the repeal of the tax. The per centage on tobacco is also small, especially when it is considered that the duty is paid upon unmanufactured tobacco, and is, consequently, a tax upon a raw material. Upon sugar Mr. Baxter believes there is no extra cost, as the trade sells that article without profit. This may be true of retail grocers, who make their profit by increasing the price of their tea, but the bulk of the sugar consumed in this country passes through the hands of the refiner, who has no opportunity of obtaining a profit on any other article. There can be no doubt, whatever, that he charges interest and profit upon the capital he advances in payment of duties; it is, perhaps, difficult to ascertain the rate of profit with exactness, but it certainly cannot be beyond the mark to estimate the increased cost of the sugar tax at 10 per cent., or £574,300.

If Mr. Dudley Baxter's estimate is adopted with the addition of 10 per cent. upon sugar, it will be seen that a burden of £9,280,346 is placed upon the consumer in excess of the amount received by the Government. It must be borne in mind that this calculation takes no account of the increased cost of taxation consequent upon the habit of purchasing in small quantities. Mr. Baxter assigns as a reason for the omission, that these extreme prices arise from the habits and weaknesses of consumers, and not from taxation. It must, however, be clear that there would be no increased cost of taxation in consequence of this habit, unless commodities were taxed. The enhanced profits of traders upon the taxes they advance, are a burden upon the consumer created by the system of indirect taxation. It is difficult, moreover, to imagine by what means a labouring man, earning say 12s., a week can make his purchases otherwise than in small quantities.

In a paper read at the Annual Meeting of the British Association, in 1850,* Mr. G. R. Porter gave the result of a very careful enquiry into the retail prices of spirits, beer, and tobacco. British spirits being most largely consumed by the working classes, and sold in very small quantities, necessarily bear a high rate of profit. The opinion of several distillers was ascertained, and Mr. Porter arrived at the conclusion that every gallon consumed cost the purchaser three times the amount of the duty. This, he estimates, is also the case with rum, the class of consumers being the same, and the means of distribution nearly, if not wholly, identical. Brandy being, for the most part, drunk by persons not of the working classes, as that term is generally but somewhat arbitrarily understood, and being sold much more frequently than British spirits in quantities of two

---

* On the Self-Imposed Taxation of the Working Classes. Printed for private circulation. See also Transactions of the Association, vol. 19, pp. 101-103.

gallons and upwards, does not afford so large a per centage of profit. A considerable quantity is sold, however, in small quantities, and it cannot be considered, according to Mr. Porter, an over estimate, averaging the quantities sold in two gallons and upwards with that sold at inns and public-houses by the glass, to fix 50 per cent. as the rate of profit upon import duty and cost. It is true that these calculations were made nearly twenty years since, but there is no reason to suppose that any change has taken place in the rate of profit upon these articles since that time.

The following tables show the result of Mr. Porter's estimate as affecting 1868-9:—

	Quantity charged. Gallons.	Duty. £	Wholesale cost exclusive of duty. £	Total wholesale cost. £
British Spirits	21,930,393	10,965,195	2,741,299	13,706,494
Rum	3,875,046	1,969,201	484,380	2,453,581
Brandy	3,347,563	1,743,522	1,087,957	2,831,479
Geneva	134,877	70,253	15,735	85,988
Other sorts, Foreign	1,007,088	524,527	100,708	625,235
	30,294,967	15,272,698	4,430,079	19,702,777

The above calculation is based upon the following estimate of prices:—British spirits and rum, 2s. 6d. per gallon; brandy, 6s. 6d. per gallon; Geneva, 2s. 4d. per gallon; other sorts, 2s. per gallon. The prices for foreign and colonial spirits are based upon the prices in the Annual Statement of the Board of Trade for 1868; British spirits have been averaged at

2s. 6d., which the author believes to be a liberal estimate. In every instance the prices fixed are over rather than under the average.

	Retail price. £	Profit upon total wholesale cost. £	Rate of profit per cent.	Profit charged on duty. £
British Spirits	32,895,585	19,189,091	139	15,241,621
Rum	5,907,603	3,454,022	140	2,756,881
Brandy	4,247,218	1,415,739	50	871,761
Geneva	128,982	42,994	50	35,126
Other Foreign Spirits	1,573,581	948,346	151	792,035
	£44,752,969	£25,050,192		£19,697,424

In this table the retail profit on Geneva is supposed to be the same as on brandy, and of the inferior foreign spirits imported principally from Hamburg the same as on British spirits. It appears, therefore, according to estimates based upon Mr. Porter's calculations, that the cost of collecting £15,272,698 of revenue from spirits, in addition to the salaries and expenses of the revenue department, is £19,697,424.

Mr. Porter also enters into minute calculations respecting the manufacture and profits of the tobacco trade. He estimates the latter at 50 per cent. upon the cost of the tobacco as imported and the duty paid thereon, adding " a moderate increase to defray all the expenses of manufacture, and the charges attendant upon the retailing of an article, nearly the whole of which is paid for in copper coins." As the heavy duty upon tobacco must be paid before the manufacturer is allowed to manipulate it, there can be no doubt that the profit upon the tax is equal to that charged upon the tobacco, and may be fairly estimated at 50 per cent. or £3,271,230. It appears, therefore, from these calculations, that the extra cost of collecting the duties on spirits and tobacco in 1868-9, beyond the salaries and expenses paid by the Treasury, was £22,968,654, and that these duties imposed a burden on the taxpayer of £44,783,813, of which the Treasury received only £21,815,159, or less than one-half the amount actually paid by the consumer.

When it is considered that the purchaser of a taxed article has to pay the accumulated profits of importers or manufacturers, wholesale dealers, and retailers; that the taxes upon sugar, tobacco, and malt are levied upon raw materials, or at a very early stage of manufacture; and that our existing duties are derived to so large an extent from taxes on commodities, which all classes are in the habit of purchasing in small quantities; it must be apparent that the increased cost to the consumer becomes a very heavy burden. If the very moderate estimate of 25 per cent. is adopted it will be seen that the £40,000,000 collected by Customs and Excise costs the public £10,000,000 beyond the amount paid into the Exchequer. That the actual cost is much heavier than 25 per cent. upon the amount of the tax must be evident to any one who examines the figures already quoted; which take no account, moreover, of the influence of such taxes in diminishing trade and employment. They are two-edged weapons, taking an undue per centage from the income of the people, and preventing, in so far as they are restraints upon trade, any increase in the amount of income received.

CHAPTER XXV.

CONCLUDING OBSERVATIONS.

Two questions remain for consideration—the comparative pressure of taxation upon various descriptions of income and property, and its economic results. As respects the former it is a difficult task to apportion exactly the amounts paid by real property, by personalty, and by industrial incomes. The following table gives an approximate result, which it is believed will be found to be tolerably accurate.

	£
Real Property:—	
Land tax, succession duty, schedule A of income tax; half the stamps, law fees, game, racehorse, and dog licenses, surcharges, and assessed taxes; one-third the inhabited house duty	8,000,000
Personal Property:—	
Probate and legacy duty, half game, racehorse, and dog licenses, and schedule C of income tax	4,900,000
Trades, Professions, and Employments:—	
Licenses, except brewers, and maltsters, charged to consumption; marine insurances; patents; income tax, schedules B, D, E; two-thirds inhabited house duty; half stamps, assessed taxes, and surcharges	9,500,000
Consumption:—	
Customs and excise and stamp duties on commodities; brewers' and maltsters' licenses	40,000,000
Additional 25 per cent. on ditto	10,000,000
	£72,400,000

In the above calculation allowance has been made for the Fire Insurance Duties, Tax on Corn, and other taxes repealed in 1869. The estimate of stamps and other taxes upon real property, excepting such as are distinctly separate in the accounts, is believed to be in excess of the actual proportion.

The great difficulty in ascertaining the comparative presssure of taxation on different classes arises from that large portion which is assessed by taxes on commodities. Of the 40,000,000 so levied, or, including the estimated addition for collection of 25 per cent., £50,000,000, the duties on wine and gold and silver plate can alone be described as paid entirely by the upper and middle classes. These amount to £1,990,000, leaving £48,000,000, in round numbers, to be apportioned between industrial, trading, and propertied incomes.

It is not necessary to enter into a minute enquiry in order to arrive at the solution of this problem; the facts of the case lie on the surface. With the exceptions already named, all our duties of Customs and Excise are levied upon articles of universal consumption, some of which are used most extensively by the poorer classes. The rich are not able to consume more of these commodities than the poor, as far, at least, as physical appetite is concerned. It must, therefore, be obvious that the chief pressure of this portion of our fiscal system falls upon the most numerous class, upon those who have the smallest means with which to make their purchases, and who have no property but their labour. This fact was acknowledged by the late Sir Robert Peel.* Speaking in reference to families, the head of which earned less than 30s. a week, he said:—"It is inevitable with a system of indirect taxation that they must pay heavily; but I know, if the burden presses unjustly upon them, it is from no want of sympathy on the part of the gentlemen of England; it is, however, inevitable. We must raise a great part of our taxation by indirect taxes, and the burden will be unequally distributed." It is possible that the owners of wage-incomes, when they come to understand thoroughly the pressure of indirect taxation, may not be content with mere sympathy, but may endeavour to ascertain whether a system of taxation which presses unjustly upon them is really inevitable.

It is not however in the mere pressure of indirect taxation upon the working classes, nor in its increased cost, consequent upon the profits advanced for duties, that it is most burdensome. Every tax ought " to keep out of the pockets of the people as little as possible, over and above what it brings into the public treasury of the State."† If there is any lesson to be learnt from the fiscal history of the last half century it is that taxes levied upon commodities, whether by

---

* Speech on the Corn Laws, March 27th, 1846.
† Wealth of Nations, Book v., Chap. ii, Part ii.

means of duties of Customs or Excise, or in any other form, are a restraint upon trade, that they hinder the creation of wealth, lessen the demand for labour, and, as a natural consequence, keep out of the pockets of the people far more than they bring into the treasury of the State. Every relaxation of our fiscal system has been followed by a marked increase in our trade, manufactures, and employment; every increase in duties on commodities has diminished trade. The reduction in the price which results from repeal of duty increases the home market for other articles, while the augmented imports of foreign products are attended by a corresponding demand abroad for our own manufactures. It has been the policy of releasing Imports from taxation, which has extended trade and increased the Exports of British Produce and Manufactures, from £47,000,000 in 1842 to £179,000,000 in 1868. If we desire a further development of our industry, and a revival of trade and employment, they will be found in the further removal of restrictions upon freedom of exchange.

There are few subjects which have given rise to more controversy than that of the incidence of taxation. It was held by John Locke, by the French Economists of the last century, from Quesnay down to Turgot, and in our own day by Dr. Chalmers, that all taxation, however levied, falls ultimately upon rent. This opinion is not held by Adam Smith or the principal modern economists. The conclusions of the

French economists are summed up by Mr. Pollard-Urquhart* in the following sentence:—"The whole of the taxation of a country, in what manner soever it is levied, or by whomsoever it is paid in the first instance, comes ultimately from the revenues of the landowners, either as a direct deduction from their rents, or by depressing the value of their properties to an equal amount."

In considering this proposition care must be taken to distinguish between rent, properly so called, and that portion of the payment commonly designated rent, which consists of the profits of capital invested either in agricultural improvements, or in the construction of dwellings and other buildings. The latter payment stands upon precisely the same footing as the profits of capital invested in any other business. In a paper read by Mr. Pollard-Urquhart at the York Meeting of the Social Science Association, in 1864, it is stated that the amount of property taxed under Schedule A in the previous year was, in round numbers, £140,000,000. This, however, included rent paid for buildings, interest upon capital laid out in improvements, and the profits of railways, iron-works, gas and waterworks, mines, and similar undertakings, since transferred to Schedule D. To the extent that such items are included under the general term rent, it must be evident that an increased rental

---

* Dialogues on Taxation, p. 51.

is precisely similar to an increased profit in any other trade or employment.

There can be no doubt that injudicious taxes prevent the growth of rent; but they also diminish profits and reduce wages. The Income Tax returns for Great Britain, as far as the same items can be compared, show the following result :*—

	Amount of Income Assessed.		
	1842-3 £	1864-5 £	Increase. £
Lands, Houses, Tithes, Manors, and Fines	86,661,944	118,737,072	32,075,128
Quarries, Mines, Ironworks, Fisheries, Canals, and Railways	6,846,256	23,744,892	16,898,636
Trades, Professions, & Employments	71,330,344	110,367,232	39,036,888

It will be obvious that the increase in houses arises partly from profit upon the capital employed in building, and that part of the increased rent of lands is the profit upon capital invested by landlords in agricultural improvements. It is the remaining portion only which can strictly be designated rent.

The increase appears to be on lands, houses, &c., about 37 per cent.; on quarries, mines, railways, &c., 246 per cent.; and on profits of trades and professions, 54 per cent. A similar result would doubtless follow

---

* Real Property Return; Session 1845, No. 102. Property and Income Tax Return; Session 1852, No. 399. Tenth Inland Revenue Report, 1866. App. lix—lxi.

any further remission of indirect taxation; rent and profits would both share the advantage.

The case is by no means different when considered in respect to the effect of taxation upon labour. High duties of customs and excise increase the prices of commodities, and by limiting exchange diminish the demand for labour. The effect upon the wage-receiving classes is therefore two-fold, and this is an incident of taxation which it is impossible for them to transfer to holders of property. If an artificial scarcity is produced, the labourer is compelled to increase the number of hours he works per day, in order to obtain subsistence. It is true this process increases pauperism and consequently adds to the poor rates, which are ultimately a deduction from rent. The peculiar incidence of taxation upon labour cannot, however, be transferred to the shoulders of the landed interest. Every section of the community is affected by injudicious taxation; rent, profits, and wages are all diminished by fiscal hindrances to freedom of exchange.

In like manner, the whole community is advantaged by the removal of such burdens. The workman experiences a fresh demand for labour, and enjoys an advance of wages; the capitalist finds new and profitable undertakings in which to embark his capital; and the landlord, though perhaps the last to receive his share of the benefit thus conferred, enjoys the most permanent advantage. Capital and labour employed in commerce and manufactures (in addition

Q

to the profits and wages earned by the capitalist and labourer) augment the value of real property, quite irrespective of any effort on the part of the landlords. They enjoy what may be called a spontaneous increase as far as any efforts of their own are concerned, and may fairly be expected to contribute towards the public requirements a larger per centage of their incomes than the capitalist and labourer by whom this augmented wealth is created.

It is frequently urged that the transfer of taxation from commodities to property is injurious to the interests of those who own the soil. If such transfer were productive of no increase in rent, there might be some force in the argument, but, inasmuch as every relief afforded to trade and industry creates an addition to the rent enjoyed by the landlords, it must be obvious that the repeal of burdens upon trade and industry, although obtained by an additional tax on rent, is not a penalty upon the propertied classes, but a profitable investment. It surely can be no hardship to pay a direct tax, the effect of which is to create an increased income for the class by whom it is paid. Taxes upon production and consumption are far more onerous in their incidence upon the landlords than taxes upon their property, inasmuch as the operation of the former is to diminish the amount of income which they would otherwise enjoy.

It is alleged that modern legislation has relieved the consumers of commodities at the expense of the owners of real property. This, however, is not the fact; since the year 1842 taxation upon the luxuries of the rich has been almost entirely repealed; taxation upon articles consumed by the masses of the population remains. Silks, velvets, jewellery, and other articles of luxury are now exempt from duty; tea, coffee, sugar, spirits, malt, and tobacco, all of which are necessarily consumed most largely by the most numerous class, constitute, at the present time, as they did before the era of tariff reforms, the main sources from which the bulk of our taxation is derived. The repeal of the window duty and of the tax on fire insurances, and the re-adjustment of the assessed taxes upon horses, carriages, and servants, have been a relief to the propertied classes, not to those whose only property is their labour.

It has been already shown that a system of taxation which presses heavily upon the wage-receiving class is also prejudicial to the interests of the landlord and the capitalist. The inevitable result of the artificial increase in price which is created by customs and excise is to diminish employment, to restrict the field for the profitable investment of capital, and to lessen the rental which would otherwise accrue to the landlords. It is entirely different in its effects from that increase in price which, notwithstanding immense foreign supplies, has taken place in many articles, and has been caused by the increased ability of the people to purchase such commodities.

The great end to be attained, in the levy of taxation, is to adjust the burden so as to place the fewest possible restraints upon industry. Such a policy is not only wise as respects the community generally, but it is also just as respects the incidence of taxation upon its various sections. No one can be said to be injured by the payment of any tax which ensures freedom for industry and security for property, unless it be excessive in amount or injurious in its economic effects. The premium necessary to ensure against loss by fire, or at sea, is paid without a complaint; if our taxes were levied upon equally sound principles, there would be as little reason to complain of them. Much has been accomplished during the last quarter of a century in the removal of injurious and oppressive taxes, but much remains to be done.

It is now ten years since the last great revision of the tariff, in 1860; since that period the duties upon tea and sugar have been reduced, and the remaining tax upon corn has been abolished. A further revision of our fiscal system is now eminently desirable, in the interests not only of our foreign, but our domestic commerce. The artificial prices, created by taxation upon the necessaries and comforts of life, lessen the purchasing power of the masses of the population, while, at the same time, they diminish the demand for their labour, and affect both the profits of capital and rent of land. The true principles upon which taxation should be based, in order to inflict the least injury upon all classes, was well described by Lord Palmerston in the following words* :—" If we are obliged to call upon any class to make for the public service a sacrifice of a large portion of their incomes, whether arising from commerce, from professions, or from labour, that very fact is the strongest possible reason why we should endeavour to enable them to make that remainder, which we leave to them, go as far as it possibly can in procuring for them, according to their respective situations in life, the necessaries, the conveniences, or the luxuries which they may wish to enjoy."

---

* Corn Law Debate, March 27th, 1846.

CHAPTER XXVI.

SUPPLEMENTARY. THE BUDGET OF 1870.

The preceding chapters were written, and nearly the whole of them were in type, before the introduction of Mr. Lowe's second Budget. In the year 1869 he converted a deficiency into a surplus by an alteration in the collection of the Income and Assessed Taxes, which enabled him to reduce instead of increasing taxation. This operation, although it was a relief to the taxpayer, was severely criticised by some of his political opponents, who were, however, effectually silenced by the surplus of £7,870,000, which enabled the Government to defray liabilities, on account of the Abyssinian Expedition, amounting to £4,300,000, without imposing any additional taxation, and to reduce the funded and unfunded debt by the sum of £3,284,600. It was his good fortune to announce, in the financial statement of the present year, an expected surplus of £4,337,000, which he proposed to increase to £4,487,000, by the substitution of fire-arm licenses for game certificates. Of this surplus the sum of £190,000 was employed in payment of the increased interest payable upon terminable annuities created for the reduction of the debt, thus reducing the available surplus to £4,297,000.

In the appropriation of this large sum to the remission of taxation, Mr. Lowe acted upon the following principles:—the repeal of small and unproductive taxes, the simplification of the Revenue Laws, and the reduction of taxation, both direct and indirect, without destroying any considerable branch of the revenue. The following is a summary of the changes he proposed, in his own words:—*

"The licenses for foot hawkers which are abolished from the 1st of October, will cost us £16,000 this year; the abolition of licenses for paper makers, soap makers, watch case makers, still makers, and playing card dealers, involves a remission of £6,000; the abolition of stamps on hailstorm, cattle, boiler, and plate glass insurance from the 1st of July, involves a remission of £1,000. The revision of duties under the Stamps Consolidation Bill, which is to take effect from the 1st of January 1871, will involve a remission of £50,000; in impressed stamps for postage on printed matter, abolished from the 1st of October, we remit £60,000; in the rate of postage on printed matter and newspapers, which is reduced one-half from the 1st of October, we remit £125,000; by the alteration of the duty on railways we remit £108,000; by taking a penny in the pound off the income tax we remit £1,250,000; and by reducing one-half the duty on sugar and molasses we take off £2,310,000. The surplus we have to deal with being £4,297,000 and the remissions amounting to £3,966,000, there will remain a net surplus of £331,000."

The remission of one-half the Sugar Duty was unquestionably the most important feature of the

---

* Financial Statement, 1870, R. J. Bush, pp. 32-23.

budget, and, although it formed an appropriate climax to Mr. Lowe's financial statement, may fairly claim the first place in consideration here. The following is the new scale of duties :*—

		s.	d.
Refined Sugar, per cwt.		6	0
First Class ,,		5	8
Second Class ,,		5	3
Third Class ,,		4	9
Fourth Class ,,		4	0
Fifth Class, or Molasses ,,		1	9

In allusion to the demand for the total repeal of this duty, recommended by the President of the Board of Trade, Mr. Lowe said:—"I wish it to be clearly understood that, in making this proposal, I am not preparing the way for either further reduction or for abolition, but that I have gone as far as I intend, and make this declaration in order to give stability to the trade, and free it from periodical annoyance, owing to apprehensions of change." It is, therefore, clear that the advocates of a Free Breakfast Table have no reason to rely upon the sympathies of the present Chancellor of the Exchequer. It is, however, possible that he may change his mind. In 1844 Sir Robert Peel said respecting the Corn Laws:†—"I must give my solemn and unqualified opposition to this proposal for the immediate removal of the present protection to agriculture;" in 1845 he made the following

---

* Financial Statement, 1870, p. 32.
† Speech on Mr. Villiers' Motion. June 26th, 1844.

important admission :*—" if the doctrine is good for corn it is good for everything else ;" and in 1846, he proposed the repeal of the Corn Laws. The convictions of Ministers of the Crown are generally influenced by the growth of public opinion; whenever the constituencies demand the repeal of this tax, either Mr. Lowe, or some other Chancellor of the Exchequer, will be found to comply with their request.

It must be evident that a mere reduction of the duty does not remove the objections which have been already advanced against this tax. The sugar question is one of great importance, not merely as affecting an article of large consumption in this country, but in relation to our foreign commerce. The United Kingdom is in possession of every facility for carrying on a large trade in this important article. In our Colonial Possessions the growth of sugar may be developed to an almost unlimited extent; in this country there are facilities for refining equal to those possessed in any other part of the world, while the extent of our shipping gives us great advantage in the pursuit of a trade, in which facility of transit is so important an ingredient. Notwithstanding the possession of all these advantages, it is a noteworthy fact that our export of sugar is insignificant, in comparison with that of other tropical products. The Board of Trade Returns show that in 1868 our exports of sugar

---

* Corn Law Debate. June 10th, 1845.

formed 2 per cent. of our imports, while, in the case of tea, they formed 22 per cent., and in that of coffee 77 per cent. The solution of this problem will, in all probability, be found in the fact that, while our export of sugar is restricted by the duty, the import and export trade in tea and coffee is perfectly free from any such hindrance to trade.

It is not merely in respect to our Exports that the sugar duty has a prejudicial effect upon employment, but also in relation to the home market. The Board of Trade returns show that during the five years ending 1868 there was an increase of 170 per cent. in the import of refined sugar, as compared with the five years ending 1863, while the increase in raw sugar was only 10 per cent; in the export of British refined sugar there was an increase of 9 per cent. If our refiners had been able, during the above period, to compete with those of other countries upon an equal footing, subject only to such advantages as are naturally enjoyed in each country, there would be no ground of complaint; the import of refined sugar would be an unquestionable advantage. Such, however, has not been the case; Foreign Governments, under the guise of a drawback, endeavoured to foster their export trade by means of bounties, and thus enabled their producers to compete with ours, not merely in foreign markets but in the United Kingdom. It was to put an end to this state of things that the convention of the 8th November, 1864, was signed in

Paris, and a series of experiments were then commenced with the view of ascertaining the basis upon which drawbacks should in future be allowed by the parties to the Convention. In the year 1867, the Commissioners of Customs announced the final settlement of the question, but deferred, until the following year, any description of the alterations thereby introduced into our scale of duties, a promise which to the present time has not been fulfilled.*

The basis of the duties and drawbacks fixed by the treaty is the quantity of pure sugar which can be obtained from different qualities and descriptions of raw sugar. A little consideration will show that a drawback upon this basis is not a full equivalent for the advance of duty. The present rate upon raw sugar is about 20 per cent. ad valorem, and it is therefore necesssary for the refiner to increase the capital employed in his business to that extent. The drawback allowed being calculated according to the amount of duty paid, it is obvious that the interest and profit upon this capital become a charge upon the refiner, which he recovers from the consumer. In proportion as the rate of taxation levied upon sugar is high or low this effect of the duty is more or less prejudicial, and an illustration of this fact may be found in the removal of some branches of industry, in

---

* Ninth Customs Report, pp. 39—40. Tenth ditto. pp. 47—49. Eleventh ditto. pp. 51—52.

connection with the sugar trade, from the United Kingdom to other places, where lower duties have been imposed.

Another effect of the graduated scale of duties is to prevent the growers from sending their sugar here in the most profitable form, both for themselves and the consumer. If there were no duties, or one uniform rate, the bulk of the sugar imported would reach us either in the form of cane juice, or sugar fit for the table; in either case economy of production would be obtained, securing a reduction in price and an increased supply. In proposing the repeal of the shilling tax on Corn, Mr. Lowe said very truly:—*
" I am satisfied we shall be doing that which will greatly tend to their benefit," alluding to the poorest and most helpless class of the community, " and be laying the foundation of a great entrepôt of trade which will not only be of advantage to the mercantile classes, but which will have the equally desirable result of creating that abundance to which the existence of an entrepôt so largely contributes by circulating traffic and lowering prices." These words are quite as applicable to the case of sugar as they were to that of corn.

The reduction of the Income Tax to 4d. in the pound, the sum which, in 1865, Mr. Gladstone recommended as the ordinary permanent rate of the

---

* Financial Statement, 1869, p. 23.

tax, was generally anticipated. One or two protests were made on the ground that it would have been wiser even to increase the tax by a penny or twopence, in order to secure the entire repeal of the sugar duties. It is very questionable whether Parliament or the country would have responded to such a proposal. An injustice, which is open and palpable, invariably excites greater hostility than one which is concealed, although the latter may be the more injurious in its effects. This is especially the case when it appears in the specious and seductive form of "voluntary taxation." That the present income tax is unfair in its comparative incidence upon real and personal property, cannot be denied. It has also other objectionable features which will prevent it, unless under exceptional circumstances, from being employed in the repeal of indirect taxation. It is quite hopeless to expect the extension, unless from pressing necessity, of a tax which is condemned as unjust by a large proportion of those by whom it is paid.

The repeal of small and unproductive licenses is a measure quite in accordance with the fiscal policy of recent years. That upon foot hawkers has been enforced at considerable expense; if law expenses and the maintenance of prisoners, convicted of infringing the provisions of the law by hawking without a license, could be ascertained, it would in all probability be found that the duty has been productive of actual loss to the Exchequer. The repeal of the stamp duties on hail-storm, cattle, boiler, and plate-glass insurances, is a measure which may be justified, not merely on the grounds alleged by Mr. Lowe that the amount produced is not worth the trouble and cost of collection, but also on the ground that these imposts, like the defunct fire-insurance duty, are taxes upon prudence. The sole surviving insurance duty, that on Marine Insurances, is equally objectionable in principle, and ought to be repealed at the earliest possible opportunity.

The imposition of a tax upon guns, in the form of a license duty, will be regarded with satisfaction by all dwellers on the outskirts of the Metropolis and other large towns, if it tend to check the indiscriminate shooting of small birds which takes place, especially on Sundays and holidays, to the annoyance of the general public and, in agricultural districts, to the injury of the farmers, the small birds thus wantonly killed being the great destroyers of the numerous insects which prey upon young crops.

One of the most important features of the budget, apart from the mere question of revenue, is the consolidation of the Stamp Laws, by the reduction of the whole law, at present embodied in an enormous number of Acts, into a single Act of Parliament. The principal changes introduced are the abolition of the progressive duty levied upon deeds according to the number of words contained; the reduction of the duty on deeds, on which there is not an *ad valorem* stamp, from 35s. to 10s. and of the duty on letters of attorney from 30s. to 10s., and the abolition of the duty on the admittance of copyhold conveyances, retaining only that levied upon surrender. The bill introduced to carry into effect Mr. Lowe's proposals respecting the Stamp Duties is mainly, and of necessity, a consolidation of the existing laws, and does not deal with these complicated imposts upon their merits. The substitution of a single Act of Parliament in place of the numerous statutes by which these duties are now levied, is, however, a measure of very great importance, and will bring this branch of the revenue, yielding an annual income of above £9,000,000, into a position in which its merits and demerits may receive adequate consideration.

The abolition of the impressed stamp on newspapers along with the attendant privilege of free transmission for fifteen days, and the substitution in lieu thereof of a halfpenny postage for each transmission of a single copy of a *bonâ fide* newspaper weighing less than six ounces, will be a benefit not merely to the newspaper press but also to the public generally. The reduction of the postage on printed matter from one penny for every four ounces, or portion thereof, to one halfpenny for every two ounces, or portion thereof, and the introduction of a halfpenny card postage for messages in which secrecy is not required, are also measures of great public advantage. It is to be hoped that in carrying out these changes the Post-office authorities will take ample measures to secure due efficiency, so that communication may not be hindered by apparently increased facilities.

The gross receipts, the expenses, and net proceeds of the Post-office for the year 1868-9 appear to be as follows :—*

Receipts.	£
Postage	4,378,570
Commission on Money Orders	175,010
Newspaper Stamps, collected by the Inland Revenue	115,987
	4,669,567

Expenditure.		
Cost of Collection :—		
Postage	3,077,526	
Money Orders	121,037	
Manufacture :—		
Of Postage Stamps charged by Inland Revenue	32,330	
Newspaper Stamps (estimated)	4,500	
Packet Service	1,096,338	
		4,331,731
Net Revenue		337,836

According to Mr. Lowe's estimate the abolition of the impressed stamp on newspapers will involve a loss to the revenue of £120,000, and the reduction of the rate on printed matter a further loss of £250,000, making a total of £370,000, or an excess of £32,000

---

* Return " Taxes and Imposts," Sess. 1869, No. 427. Finance Accounts, 1868-9. pp. 76-77. Civil Service Estimates, 1868-9, Revenue Departments, p. 32.

beyond the net revenue of the Post Office. In these estimates, however, no allowance appears to be made for the increased business which will be transacted in consequence of a reduction in the rates of charge.

The only serious objection to the alterations proposed in the transit of newspapers and printed matter has reference to the peculiar facilities afforded to the former, and the favour shown to certain newspapers. If the Post Office is able to carry six ounces of printed matter for a half-penny in the shape of a single newspaper, it may fairly be presumed that it can carry, at the same rate, a packet containing six ounces of newspapers irrespective of the number of copies contained in such packet, and that printed matter of any description can be carried on the same terms. The vexed question of what constitutes a newspaper, which has already occasioned extensive and costly litigation in relation to the compulsory newspaper stamp, is reopened by this measure. All the former difficulties of the Post Office, in connection with the transmission of newspapers, are revived, throwing an amount of labour upon the department which, in all probability, will seriously impede its successful working. A far more simple and practicable method would be the levy of two distinct rates for printed matter—a quick rate which would be generally used for newspapers and packets requiring speed, and a slow rate for books and other printed matter, in respect to which a delay in the delivery is not of such importance.

The proposal of the Budget which excited the

greatest hostility, and which was eventually withdrawn, was the commutation of the duty of 5 per cent. upon first and second class passengers into a duty of 1 per cent. upon the gross receipts of railways. In repealing the other taxes on locomotion in 1869, Mr. Lowe, held out an expectation that, in consideration of some new arrangements respecting the conveyance of the mails and of troops, he would be able in a future Budget to relieve railways from special taxation. In the Budget for 1870 he acted like the celebrated characters in Macbeth, who were said to

> "Keep the word of promise to our ear,
> And break it to our hope!"

The practical working of the proposed change would have relieved certain railways at the expense of others; some passenger railways would have benefited considerably by the change; those whose traffic consists mainly of goods, especially mineral lines, would have been mulcted in a very heavy addition to their present taxation; while several of the larger railways, which had been allowed by Parliament, in consideration of reductions in the rates of fares, to charge the railway passenger duty upon their customers, would have been unable to do so, and the duty would have been transferred to the shareholders. It is possible to collect a tax of 5 per cent. upon first and second class passengers, but quite impossible to recover 1 per cent. upon gross receipts.

The main reason urged by Mr. Lowe, in support of

the special taxation of railways was the assertion that "they enjoy a certain qualified kind of monopoly," and, in favour of this theory, the high authority of the "Economist" newspaper has been enlisted, on the ground that the State has a right to share the profits of a monopoly. It would appear from such an argument that railways enjoyed a rate of profit in excess of that of other trades, instead of being, as described by Mr. Lowe himself,* an "interest, which has made everybody's fortune except its own." According to the estimate of Mr. Dudley Baxter,† which is based upon Parliamentary returns, the average rate of dividend on ordinary share capital, which bears the whole weight of this taxation, is 3 per cent., the burden imposed by local rates and Government duty being equivalent to nearly 16 per cent. upon such income, besides Income Tax and the Probate and Legacy Duties. From this special burden the debenture capital and the preference stock, the average rate of interest on which is more than $4\frac{1}{2}$ per cent., are exempt. There are railways which pay no interest upon either their original or their preference capital; it certainly cannot be just to levy upon the holders of such unproductive property a special tax, from which they are now exempt.

The doctrine that the State has a right to participate

---

* Financial Statement, 1869, p. 29.
† The Taxation of the United Kingdom, p. 103 104

in the profits of a monopoly has a far wider significance than the advocates of its application to the case of railways intend. Rent is an effect of monopoly,* in which, according to the principle laid down by the authorities just quoted, the State has a right to participate. In connection with this argument, as employed in favour of a special tax upon railways, it may be well to consider the effect they have produced upon rent. In a paper read by Mr. Dudley Baxter before the Statistical Society,† it is shown that "it is almost impossible to construct a railway through a new district, of fair agricultural capabilities, without saving to the landowner and farmer alone the whole cost of the line." Notwithstanding this great and unquestionable advantage, landowners, as a rule, have claimed and obtained heavy sums by way of compensation for the compulsory sale of land required for the construction of railways, and have thus derived a twofold advantage from that interest upon which exclusively a special taxation is now advocated.

The railway passenger duty was first imposed in 1832, at the rate of one halfpenny for every four passengers; in 1842, it was altered to 5 per cent. upon the gross receipts of passenger traffic; and in 1844, when Parliament compelled railway companies to carry third-class passengers at a penny a mile, that

---

* Mill's Principles of Political Economy, Book II., c. xvi.
† Journal of the Statistical Society. December, 1866.

portion of their passenger traffic was made exempt from duty.* The introduction of such a tax was opposed by Mr. Hume, on the ground that it was unsound in principle to tax locomotion. The only plea upon which it was defended by the Chancellor of the Exchequer (Lord Althorp), and the Secretary to the Treasury (Mr. Spring-Rice), was that the State could not afford to dispense with the duty upon stage coaches, with which railways would compete.† The original duty upon railway passengers was levied in the same form as that upon stage coaches, another proof that the two imposts were identical in their origin. The growth of railways having reduced the stage carriage duty to an amount which was hardly worth collection, it was repealed, and a new pretext is now discovered for perpetuating the tax upon railway passengers.

It is somewhat amusing to find the argument of monopoly advanced, at a time when the great complaint of many of our railways is the encouragement by Parliament of excessive competition. On every considerable route there are competing lines, which have reduced fares, and increased facilities for traffic; in the conveyance of goods, railways have, in many instances, to meet the competition of canals and steam vessels, both of which are exempt from taxa-

---

* First Inland Revenue Report, pp. 16-17.

† Hansard's Parliamentary Debates, July 1832.

tion, and in the case of the latter have no permanent way to provide, maintain, and renew. It must be apparent that the "certain qualified kind of monopoly" enjoyed by railways is of a very peculiar kind, the qualifications being so numerous and effective as to deprive the shareholders of any one of the advantages which usually attend the possession of a monopoly. It may, no doubt, be urged in justification of a tax upon railway traffic, that stage coaches are liable to the carriage duty, and the tax on horses. Railways, however, are assessed to local taxation, upon the permanent way, which they construct themselves, while the owners of other conveyances are liable to no such burden. The assessment of railways to the local rates must be more than an equivalent for the carriage duty levied upon other public conveyances.

The following table shows the amount produced by the stage carriage and railway passenger duties in 1833, the first complete year during which the latter tax was received; in 1842, the year in which the tax was altered to 5 per cent. upon gross receipts; in 1844 the year when "parliamentary" traffic was freed from duty; and in 1868-9*

	Railway Duty. £	Stage Carriages. £	Total £
1833	6,131	458,028	464,159
1842	153,831	287,672	441,503
1844	167,854	242,728	410,582
1868-9	460,208	49,030	509,238

* Report of Commissioners of Inland Revenue, 1870, vol 2, pp. 29, 32.

It is clear, from these returns, that the railway passenger duty had replaced the stage carriage duty as a source of revenue, and that the special taxes on locomotion cannot be said to be repealed so long as a tax upon railway traffic is maintained. The Stage Carriage Duty and the Railway Passenger Duty ought to have been repealed at the same time.

The proposals of the Budget, however, involved three distinct changes: the reduction of the existing duty; the renewal of the duty upon third-class traffic, which had been repealed in 1844; and the imposition, for the first time, of a tax upon the transit of goods. If it had been intended simply to relieve railways from taxation, a mere reduction of the duty would have been sufficient for the purpose. The Inland Revenue Commissioners had, however, another object in view; controversies had arisen between them and the companies as to the liability of certain kinds of traffic to the duty; litigation was pending or in progress, when, no doubt, the happy idea occurred to some ingenious guardian of the revenue that a legislative *coup d'état* would solve the difficulty. Hence the appearance in the Budget of the proposed tax on gross receipts, and the endeavour to upset the existing arrangement which had been justified by the Prime Minister* on the ground that "a great distinction should be drawn between the locomotion of luxury and pleasure, and that which is of necessity." The

---

* Financial Statement, 1866.

difficulty with the revenue authorities as to the assessment of the present tax, relates solely to excursion traffic at rates very much below the Parliamentary limit of a penny a mile. Whether such traffic, especially in its relation to inhabitants of large towns, is locomotion of luxury and pleasure, or of necessity, may be left for casuists to determine; and, until they have done so, the zeal of the Inland Revenue Commissioners may very reasonably be allowed to rest.

A tax of 1 per cent. upon the gross receipts of railways has a very modest unassuming aspect, but presents vastly different features upon a close examination. In the first place, it has very much the appearance of an additional leg to that metaphorical table of which Mr. Lowe once spoke. One per cent., upon an emergency may be raised to 2, 3, or even 5 per cent., by a Chancellor of the Exchequer engaged in the pursuit, well described by Sir Robert Peel, of fishing for a Budget. In the second place, a tax of 1 per cent. upon gross receipts is a tax of 2 per cent. upon net earnings, the average working expenses of railways being fully 50 per cent. In the third place, the whole burden of the tax would fall upon less than half the capital invested, and become practically an additional income tax upon holders of ordinary stock of fully 4 per cent. According to the latest return,[*] the capital of railways was distributed as follows :—

---

[*] Lords' Return, "Railways." Session 1868, No. 292.

			£
Preference Stock	...	..	143,209,357
Debenture Stock	...	...	15,637,117
Debenture Loans	...	...	110,392,559
			269,239,033
Ordinary Stock	...	...	233,023,854
Total	...	...	£502,262,887

It is on the amount invested in ordinary shares, forming about 46 per cent. of the total capital, and paying an average dividend of 3 per cent., that the whole weight of such an impost would fall. In the case of railways, which pay no dividend to their ordinary shareholders, it would amount to a confiscation of the property of the preference shareholders, and in that of some lines, which are unable to meet the claims of their preference shareholders, to a similar operation in respect to the interest due to their creditors. It was no doubt quite competent for Parliament to impose conditions upon railways at the time of granting powers for their construction; it was then at the option of the companies to accept their Acts upon the terms imposed or to refuse them, but it is difficult to justify the imposition of a special burden, falling upon capital invested in loans or preference shares, on the faith of existing arrangements. Facility of internal communication is, moreover, an important element of national prosperity, which ought not to be interfered with by exceptional fiscal arrangements.

A concession was made to the agricultural interest by according the privilege, under restrictions as to the distance from a malt kiln at which the process may be carried on, of steeping barley for the purpose of feeding cattle. The proposal to convert the Malt Tax into a license duty upon brewers was rejected on account of the greater difficulty involved in collecting such an impost, owing to the increased number of persons from whom it would have to be received, and the impossibility of imposing it upon private brewers.

The nature of taxation and the true principle upon which it should be based formed the subject of the concluding portion of Mr. Lowe's financial statement. He does not agree either with those who hold that all taxation should be direct, or with those who would advocate the exclusive employment of indirect taxation. According to his theory the imposition of taxation is the distribution of so much misery, which it is his function to make as tolerable as possible, by spreading it over a number of articles. Taxation being a payment to the State for services rendered, it is difficult to see why it should be more productive of misery than the payment of rent, of premiums upon insurance, or any other contribution in return for the performance of a service. Mr. Lowe admits fully the great advantage of direct taxation, but condemns it as the sole source of revenue, because the payment of it is compulsory. He further alleges that you compel a man to pay it when payment may be ruin; if, however, it is fairly levied, according to the amount of property owned by each taxpayer, it is difficult to understand in what respect this allegation can be sustained. No one complains that he is ruined by any similar payment; it would have been more accurate to describe the function of the Chancellor of the Exchequer as that of securing an adequate contribution from each taxpayer in proportion to his means, as an equivalent for the advantages he derives from the existence of Civil Government. The doctrine now advanced by Mr. Lowe is very similar to the one laid down, in 1857, by Sir G. C. Lewis, which was at once disclaimed by Mr. Gladstone.* It has also been described by the author of the Biglow Papers in the following lines:—

> "I du believe in any plan
>   O' levyin' the taxes,
> Ez long ez, like a lumberman,
>   I git jest wut I axes:
> I go free-trade thru thick an' thin,
>   Because it kind o' rouses,
> The folks to vote,—an' keeps us in
>   Our quiet custom-houses."

Mr. Lowe assumes that the repeal of indirect taxation would throw a heavy pressure elsewhere, and lays down the sound principle that "everybody should contribute, however small his contribution, to the revenue." The latter doctrine is held with equal firmness by the advocates of direct taxation; the question at issue between them and their opponents, in respect to this branch of the subject, being whether

---

* Fiscal Legislation. Longmans. pp. 72–73.

indirect taxation does, or does not, place the heaviest burden upon those who have the smallest means. The opinion that the repeal of duties of customs and excise would, of necessity, place an undue burden upon any class of the community is one which they deny, the lesson which they gather from our past financial experience being that no class of the community would derive greater benefit from the substitution of direct for indirect taxation than owners of property of every description That indirect taxation is wasteful and extravagant, Mr. Lowe has fully admitted; its one advantage, in his eyes, is the fact that it is optional, a condition which is certainly at variance with the sound principle, advocated by all political economists, of contribution according to means of each taxpayer.

Another argument employed by Mr. Lowe in defence of his theory is the inexpediency of narrowing too much the basis of taxation and the necessity of being prepared for emergencies which will render an increased revenue inevitably necessary. No tax, whether direct or indirect, is the basis of taxation, but an instrument by means of which taxation is raised. It would be quite as reasonable to describe a pump as the basis of a water supply. There are three funds which form the basis of taxation,—rent, profits, and wages; any tax which prevents the growth of these sources of revenue narrows the basis of taxation. If it be desirable, which few will deny, to be prepared for any emergency that may arise, the best mode of ensuring such preparation is the levy of our taxation in the mode which causes the least interference with the growth of the fund, from which such increased resources must be drawn.

The great questions of controversy between the advocates of Direct and Indirect Taxation cannot be solved by reference to phenomena in Natural History, which have no analogy whatever to the subject. These may, perhaps, serve to enliven a financial statement, and help to carry a budget, but are quite useless in the examination of a problem, which requires a close and careful study of its own peculiar phenomena. If it be proved by investigation into facts that any portion of our fiscal system imposes burdens upon the people far in excess of the amount received by the State, that it tends to diminish employment and depreciate the value of property, and that these evils far outweigh its advantages, it will be alike the duty and the interest of the community to endeavour to find some substitute, by means of which the Taxation of the United Kingdom may be placed upon a Sound and Equitable Footing.

FINIS.

EXPLANATORY REFERENCES.

Page 6. Table showing the proceeds of the Customs Revenue at different periods. The figures for the year 1815 are from McCulloch's British Empire. In the First Customs Report the amount for that year is £14,330,390, and for the year 1816 it is £11,891,563.

Page 54. Add :—" The quantity charged with duty and the amount produced, for the year 1868-9, were :—
"Quantity taxed........ 103,918,241 lbs.
Amount produced .... £2,597,980."

Page 114. Table of Stamp Duties :—The figures in the First Inland Revenue Report and the revised edition vary slightly. The figures quoted are from the First Report, omitting shillings and pence.

Page 120. Lines 3, 4, 5 :—These figures are from Parliamentary Paper, Session 1869, No. 427.

Page 145. Land Tax. The Inland Revenue Commissioners state the amount of Land Tax redeemed, to the present time, as £800,397, the difference between this amount and the balance of the sums realised in 1798 and 1869 is, no doubt, owing to the non-assessment in the last named year of personal property.

Page 149. The net receipt of the Income Tax, for the ten years ending 1816, is not given in the revised Report, published in 1870. There is, therefore, no corresponding reference for these figures.

Page 164. Table of Lands Assessed under Schedule A, 1864-65 :—The increase of "£898,483," for the year 1864-5, is over 1856-7.

Page 203. Line 17 :—After "entire remission," insert the words "during the current year." See Financial Statement, 1869, p. 29.

Page 242. Line 25 :—After "It is possible" insert "for the Railway Companies." Line 26 :—For "upon" read "from."

ADDITIONAL REFERENCES.

The First Annual Report of the Inland Revenue Commissioners being out of print, it has been considered advisable to add a table showing the corresponding references in the new and revised edition, issued since the greater part of this work was printed. In some instances the figures vary slightly in the two reports, and in others information which was contained in the original report, principally relating to taxes since repealed, has been omitted from the new and revised edition.

First Inland Revenue Report—1857.		Inland Revenue Report—1870.
Page 19.	App. p. 43.	Vol. II., p. 9.
,, 20.	pp. 3-6.	Vol. I., p. 12.
,, 24.	pp. 6, 7, 8.	Vol. I., pp. 24-26.
,, 59.	App. pp. 15, 16.	Vol. I., p. 37.
,, 92.	App. p. 22.	Vol. I., p. 94.
,, 93.	App. p. 101.	Vol. II., p. 157.
,, 98.	App. p. xxiii.	Vol. I., pp. 95.
,, 99.	App. p. ciii.	Vol. II., p. 157.
,, 113.	App. p. xcix.	Vol. II., p. 127.
,, 124.	p. 35.	Vol. I., p. 116.
,, 145.	pp. 38-39.	Vol. I., p. 112.
,, ,,	App, pp. 30-32.	Vol. II., pp. 159-160.
,, 149.	pp. 30-31.	Vol. I., pp. 120-121.
,, 151.	Second note.	Vol. II., p. 190.
,, 164.	App. p. cxxix.	Vol. II., p. 185.
,, 166.	App. p. cxxix.	Vol. II., p. 185.
,, 180.	App. pp. 130, 131.	Vol. II., pp. 186, 187.
,, 192.	App. p. cxxix.	Vol. II., pp. 185.
,, 245.	pp. 16, 17.	Vol. I., pp. 47-48.

ERRATA.

Page 23. Scotland, 1856:—for "7,715,939 gallons," read 7,175,939 gallons; Ireland, 1852:—for "4,929,512 gallons," read 4,929,572 gallons.

Page 28. Table of Imports of Rum, 1849:—for "4,479,549 gallons," read 5,306,827 gallons.

Page 35. Second Note:—for "1859," read 1868.

Page 41. Last line for "2 per cent," read 15 per cent.

Page 51. Table of Imports and Consumption of Tea, line 7:—for "1852," read 1862.

Page 57. Table of Consumption, 1842, Foreign, 1842:—for "11,219,646 lbs." read 11,219,730 lbs. Second line after Table of Rate of Duty and Consumption of Coffee:—for "60 per cent," read 38 per cent. Last line:—for "18 per cent," read 15¾ per cent.

Page 60. Note:—After "3 and 4 Wm. 4, c. 56," insert 6 and 7 Wm. 4, c. 60.

Page 61. Table of Rates of Duty on Chicory, 1861, Excise:—for "6s. 0d.," read 5s. 6d. from April 1, and 8s. 6d. from June 12.

Page 62. Table of Duty, Quantity Taxed, and Sum produced, of Chicory, Excise:—for "£4,358," read £14,358. Total, for "£108,399," read £118,399.

Page 77. Table of Malt Duties:—"32 qrs. 4 bush.," and "£41," are the quantity and amount of "Foreign," not "Isle of Man."

Page 89. Drivers of Metropolitan Public Carriages:—for "12,144," read 12,744.

Page 91. Line 11:—for "1795," read 1797.

Page 92. Line 6:—for "1806," read 1816.

Page 92. Lines 21 and 22:—for "1795," read 1797.

Page 93. Table of Probate Duties:—Property under £100 has been exempt since July, 1864.

Page 94. Table of Probate Duties:—"£700,000 to £800,000 with will annexed":—for "£15,000," read £10,500.

Page 102. Table of Amount paid for Legacy and Succession Duties:—for "£1,861,725," read £1,861,587.

Page 124. Table of House Duty :—Shops and Warehouses, for " £8,049,332," read £8,049,322.

Page 128. First Note :—for " 1846," read 1845.

Page 145, Line 19 :— for " £1,989,673," read 2,037,627. Line 20 :— for " 1,131,301," read 1,131,321. Line 21 :—for " 858,372," read 906,306.

Page 164. First Note, Tenth Inland Revenue Report :—for " p. ix.," read p. lx.

Page 167. Page 18 :—for " £55,909,000," read 55,900,000.

Page 183. Table of Income Tax Assessment, Ireland :—for " £5,927,536," read 5,926,536. Total :—for " £125,896,695," read 125,895,695.

Page 192, Lines 19, 20 :—for " The last amount assessed under the head," read The amount assessed under the last head.

Page 194. Table :—Fisheries, for " 61¾ per cent.," read 62¾ per cent.

Page 209. Second Note :—for " Inland," read Island.

Page 246. In Table of Railway Duty :—

	£		£
1842 for	" 153,831,"	read	168,957
1844 ,,	" 410,854,"	,,	177,603
1868-9 ,,	" 460,208,"	,,	500,383

Total of Railways and Stage Carriages :—

	£		£
1842 for	" 441,503,"	read	456,629
1844 ,,	" 410,582,"	,,	420,331
1868-9 ,,	" 509,238,"	,,	549,413

WORKS BY THE SAME AUTHOR.

FISCAL LEGISLATION, 1842-1865. A Review of the Financial changes of that period, and their effects upon Revenue, Trade, Manufactures, and Employment. 1 vol. 8vo. 7s. 6d.

OUR IMPORTS AND EXPORTS: with some remarks upon the BALANCE of TRADE. Also a complete analysis of the Imports and Exports of 1868, showing the respective proportions of food and other articles of consumption, raw materials, and manufactures. 8vo. sewed, 2s. 6d.

London: LONGMANS, GREEN, READER & DYER.

FREE TRADE, RECIPROCITY, AND THE REVIVERS: an Enquiry into the effects of the Free Trade Policy upon Trade, Manufactures, and Employment. Sewed 6d.

London: SIMPKIN, MARSHALL & Co.

www.ingramcontent.com/pod-product-compliance
Lightning Source LLC
Chambersburg PA
CBHW031951230426
43672CB00010B/2129